THREE RINGLING CIRCUS

A History of Sarasota, Florida, and the

Famous Ringling Brothers

SANDRA GURVIS

Pineapple Press
Palm Beach, Florida

Pineapple Press
An imprint of Globe Pequot, the trade division of
The Rowman & Littlefield Publishing Group, Inc.
4501 Forbes Blvd., Ste. 200
Lanham, MD 20706
www.rowman.com

Distributed by NATIONAL BOOK NETWORK

British Library Cataloguing in Publication Information available

Library of Congress Cataloging-in-Publication Data

Names: Gurvis, Sandra, author.
Title: Three Ringling circus : a history of Sarasota, Florida, and the famous Ringling
    Brothers / Sandra Gurvis.
Description: Palm Beach, Florida : Pineapple Press, [2024] | Includes bibliographical
    references and index.
Identifiers: LCCN 2023023196 (print) | LCCN 2023023197 (ebook) | ISBN
    9781683342984 (paperback) | ISBN 9781683342991 (epub)
Subjects: LCSH: Ringling Brothers. | Ringling Brothers Barnum and Bailey Combined
    Shows. | Ringling, John, 1866-1936. | Circus owners—United States—Biography. |
    Circus—United States—History. | Sarasota (Fla.)—History. | Sarasota (Fla.)—
    Biography
Classification: LCC GV1821.R5 G87 2024 (print) | LCC GV1821.R5 (ebook) |
    DDC 791.3092 [B]—dc23/eng/20230807
LC record available at https://lccn.loc.gov/2023023196
LC ebook record available at https://lccn.loc.gov/2023023197

Printed in India.

To my granddaughter Hope: The entire arena of life is ahead of you.
Reach for the stars and transcend your dreams.

CONTENTS

ACKNOWLEDGMENTS

Writing a nonfiction historical book is like dealing with a tsunami; without a team of "first responders," it would be almost impossible not to get swept away. I would like to thank the following people for helping me sort through the deluge of information:

At the John and Mable Ringling Museum of Art (aka The Ringling):

- **Susan O'Shea**, archival collections specialist. There are not enough words to thank Susan, who was instrumental and resourceful in sorting through the countless details involved in writing this book. I came for the material but stayed for a friendship that involved gossiping about the Ringlings and discussing the antics of our various felines.

- **Marissa Hershon**, curator of Ca' d'Zan and Decorative Arts, provided me with a wonderful and thorough "insider's tour" of Ca' d'Zan. Because it helped me see their home though John's and Mable's eyes, it provided me with further insights into their lives.

- **Peggy Williams**, assistant archivist, whose entertaining and lively tales of the Clown College and circus life in general helped inform this book.

- The **rest of the staff at The Ringling** who were more than accommodating during my many visits there. It is a beautiful and amazing place, and every time I went, I discovered something new.

I would also like to thank the **Manatee County Public Library**, which not only allowed me generous (almost two-year!) constant renewal of books on the Ringlings, "The" Ringling, and the circus but also access to its outstanding collection of historical papers on Manatee County, Sarasota, and Florida in general.

During the beginning of the process and despite the many limitations imposed by the COVID-19 pandemic, librarian **David Breakfield** provided me with copies of rare papers, letters, and other documents.

With regard to supplying and providing permission for photos, I would also like to thank the following:

- The John and Mable Ringling Museum of Art
- State Archives of Florida/Florida Memory
- State Library of Florida
- Manatee County Public Library
- Sarasota County History Center/Sarasota History Alive!
- Murray Horwitz

In the friend/colleague/pet arena, there are too many to thank who provided a sounding board and support, but I want to thank especially these folks:

- **Barbara Mandel** and her daughter **Alyssa Mandel**, who introduced me to Sarasota (Barbara) and helped show me the online library "ropes" (Alyssa).
- **Murray Horwitz**, Clown College graduate and fellow native Daytonian (Ohio), who also provided great information about the former and interesting tidbits about the latter.
- **Ana McGrath** of the New College of Florida, for her generosity in giving me a tour of the former Charles Ringling mansion as well as access to 100-year-old correspondence about the business end of the circus (and not just the animals!).
- **Bill Modrow**, head archivist at the Miami University libraries, where I worked as a college student, who introduced me to archivists and resources at Florida State University. It's good to have friends amid the "stacks"!

My cat, the late Mr. Peabody, who stuck around long enough for me to almost finish the book but who, after 14 years and multiple health problems, unexpectedly crossed the Rainbow Bridge. And my new itinerant Highlander kitten, Adrian (named after Adrian Paul, a human "Highlander"), who bolstered the motto "there can be only one" in terms of four-legged mischief and entertainment.

Last but most certainly not least, my editors:

- **Erin Turner**, who "signed" me when I moved to Florida and believed in the initial vision of the book.

- **Amy Lyons**, who temporarily took over from Erin and whom I've worked with on several previous projects.

- And especially **Lauren Younker** and **Debra Murphy**. Lauren, who was not only very patient but also responsive, insightful, and supportive, inherited the project and took it on as her own. Ditto for Debra, whose resourcefulness helped me land some all-important photos.

I think we all would agree that this book was a challenge, but I believe the end result is worth it.

INTRODUCTION

John Ringling was many things to many people. A son, brother, and uncle, whose determined individualism caused many a rift; a husband (twice), the first time harmonious, the second, the exact opposite; a shrewd businessperson, who if you asked 10 people what they thought, would likely get the same number of different opinions; and a public figure whose flashy, ornate lifestyle attracted both admiration and controversy. Yet in spite of all the fanfare and publicity, John Ringling, his brothers, and their families were essentially private people.

So how was it that I, a native of Dayton, Ohio, and author of some 18 books, covering topics ranging from Ohio history/tourist spots to business/relocation to museums to traveling with pets to (don't laugh) Paris Hilton, and even a couple of novels, drawn to John Ringling, his family, and their circus?

There are many reasons, the most obvious of which is that I moved to the Ringling mothership (aka Sarasota) in June 2020—in the middle of a pandemic, no less. So in the sense of proximity, it was a logical choice. It was also a culmination of what I've done throughout my career: Seen a need for information and tried to fill the gap. Not much has been written in recent years about the Ringlings, The Ringling (which encompasses far more than the art museum), and Sarasota in this particular combination, although there have been several excellent books:

- Karl Grismer's *The Story of Sarasota: The History of the City and County of Sarasota, Florida*
- Henry Ringling North's *The Circus Kings: Our Ringling Family Story*
- David C. Week's *Ringling: The Florida Years 1911–1936*

When I first started this project, these books were recommended to me, and I used and quoted from them extensively, along with others. The point being to represent as balanced and historically accurate a picture as possible, even if the sources contradicted each other, as sometimes happened.

I've never traveled with a circus, although at times my life has felt like one, whether it be the joyful chaos of raising two children and several cats or dealing with tragedy, such as my late son's battle with drug addiction. Having grown up in a family that supported

SANDRA GURVIS

unusual and sometimes risky (but always legal) endeavors, I also felt a kinship with the Ringling family because of their emphasis on the basic values of honesty, integrity, and hard work. My late father, who grew up in the 1920s and whose own father died in the flu pandemic of 1918, had very little while growing up, yet he managed to get a degree in optometry from Ohio State and start his own successful practice, which he had for nearly 50 years. I would like to think that I imprinted many of his habits in my career as a freelance writer who is essentially self-employed.

And like myself, who started out knowing no one and very little about the business of writing and journalism, I, like the Ringlings, had to learn from experience and figure things out as they unfolded. While there are, of course, different levels of success, a certain level of tenacity, receptiveness, and ability to distill the truth is required to endure. And Ringling is still around today, both as a museum/tourism destination and circus repurposed to meet 21st-century sensibilities. Not many families can claim that.

With this book, I tried to bring a fresh approach and perspective to the Sarasota: The Backstory, John Ringling, and his brothers as well as The Ringling itself. While this was a much more immense and challenging task than originally envisioned, if something got overlooked, was not mentioned, or was even misinterpreted (a matter of opinion, sometimes), please understand that I have done my best.

Regardless, I truly hope that you, the reader, enjoy this book and get at least some of the insight and entertainment that I received from writing it.

Sandra Gurvis
Sarasota, Florida
March 31, 2023

RING ONE
Sarasota: The Backstory

Chapter 1

Ancient Sarasota

THE FIRST "SNOWBIRDS"

During the Ice Age, about a million years ago—give or take a few 10,000—a prehistoric circus of giant mastodons, armadillos, and rhinoceros joined the early ancestors of horses, camels, beavers, and tigers in an exodus to the Sarasota area to escape the brutal cold of the northern regions.

Although approximately a third of the planet was covered in glaciers, then, as now, Florida was warm, sunny, and temperate and only a few degrees cooler than it is today, but without the hair-curling humidity. The sea level was lower and coastline farther out, with an arid climate more akin to an African savannah than, say, the giant "Mouse House" that would be constructed eons later in Orlando, about two hours north. Icebergs, some taller than the Empire State building, drifted past the coastline. "Tampa Bay was a valley with a little stream running down the middle of it, so it was a very different place," Scott Mitchell, collections manager for Florida Archaeology, told the *LA Times*.

But it was hardly a trip to Orlando's Jurassic World. "An armadillo called a glyptodont, which was the size of a small car, whacked predators with a tail resembling a spiked club," continued the *LA Times* article. "Saber-toothed cats sported 9-inch fangs—the largest of any feline in Earth's history. But beavers weighing up to 500 pounds could out-chomp them with teeth up to a foot long."

Archeological evidence has shown that Florida's and particularly Sarasota's proclivity for attracting the odd and usual began during this period. "Uncounted millions of those queer animals came to the Florida peninsula during the great migration," wrote

Karl Grismer in *The Story of Sarasota*. Digs such those in Indian Beach in the 1920s by paleontologist J. E. Moore unearthed over 70 fossil species found nowhere else in the state. Moore also discovered what some believed was a 20,000-year-old skeleton of an early Indian in nearby Phillippi Creek. At the time considered one of the oldest such artifacts ever found—although more recent studies have unearthed *Homo sapiens* remains dating as far back as 46,000–44,000 years—Moore's discovery still defies conventional wisdom that the Native Americans arrived in the area only about 12,000 years or so ago. And that was about six millennia **before** the construction of the Egyptian pyramids.

THE FIRST FLORIDIANS

Florida's original human inhabitants descended from migrants who crossed from Alaska to Eastern Asia during the Pleistocene era, back when land actually linked the two continents. Grismer, whose book was first published in 1946, called them "aborigines," while today they are known as Paleo Indians, a nod to the trendy 21st-century diet derived from their menu of unprocessed meats, fish, fruits, nuts, vegetables, and seeds. As with the settlers and hordes of tourists who followed them, they were drawn to Sarasota's attractions, including pristine beaches, plentiful wildlife/plants, and sunny weather. Then, as now, life could be easy and pleasant, compared to up North, where tribes battled each other for territory so they could hunt for food and faced starvation during long and freezing winters.

But because there were few springs, wetlands, and rivers, water was in short supply, which is where sinkholes came in handy. Rather than being feared for their ability to swallow homes and cars, they contained life-sustaining water. Both animals and humans relied on sinkholes, "not only for drinking water, but also for campsites where animals could be ambushed, butchered, and eaten," according to Sarasota History Alive! "Evidence of these campsites is found today at the bottom of rivers, such as the Aucilla River in

North Florida and sinkholes, such as Warm Mineral Springs and Little Salt Springs in Sarasota County."

Nearby Warm Mineral Springs has been particularly fruitful in yielding information about Florida's Paleo Indians. "Debris cones" located hundreds of feet beneath the surface provided an archeological treasure trove and catchall for their remains as well as the stone, bone, and ivory tools they used; animal bones; and even foodstuffs such as nuts. "To find such fragile artifacts in such a pristine state of preservation was extraordinary," stated Sarasota History Alive! W. A. "Sonny" Cockrell, an underwater archaeologist with Florida State University who started excavating the springs in the early 1970s, attributed this natural preservation to the lack of oxygen in the water.

As the climate changed, life got easier, and food and water became more plentiful. The timeline is mind boggling:

About 9,000 years ago, the glaciers began to melt as Florida's climate became warmer and wetter, and plants and animals in the region became more diverse. Between 7,000 and 6,000 years ago . . . our modern forests and wetland environments began to appear . . .

Around 4,000 years ago, as sea levels and climate approached modern conditions, native people began to depend more on wetland resources such as fish, shellfish and turtles. They also developed limited horticulture or small household gardens. Human population increased. Settlements became more seasonal and were usually located near sources of fresh water and raw chert, the stone used for making tools. These innovative and adaptive people began firing clay to make pottery for storing, preparing and serving food. (VisitFlorida.com)

The Paleo Indians were followed by the Archaic people, who lived from 7500 B.C. to 500 B.C. Around 1100 A.D. regional cultures began to develop, with populations staying in one area, where they hunted and gathered food and began to develop their own specific culture and complex societies as well as cooking utensils and hunting tools. According to Jerald Milanich's *Florida Indians and the Invasion from Europe* and archeologist Dan Hughes, the first of these regional cultures in the Sarasota area, the Manasota, were "dwellers who subsisted heavily on marine resources and lived in Sarasota from 500 B.C. to A.D. 800/1000."

"The Manasota culture was eventually replaced by what is called the Safety Harbor culture around 1000 A.D.," the article goes on. The Tocobaga tribe, the largest of this group, "lived in small villages at the northern end of Tampa Bay from 900 to the 1500s," observed the Florida State University's "Exploring Florida" website. A mostly peaceful tribe, their "houses were generally round and built with wooden poles holding up a roof of palm thatches."

Another descendent of the Paleo Indians were the Calusa, or "shell Indians," named after their proclivity for collecting shells, which they made into tools, jewelry, and hunting ornaments including spears. Fierce and warlike, the other tribes took care not to offend them, although according to Grismer's book, until the arrival of the Spaniards in the 1500s, they were mostly friendly to visiting tribes. At one point, these seafarers and hunters were some 50,000 strong and controlled most of South Florida, according to Florida State University's "Exploring Florida" website.

Still another tribe, the Timucua, lived in Northeast and North Central Florida. Because they were nomadic, they mingled freely with other tribes and were among the first to come into contact with the Spaniards when they arrived at what is now Longboat Key and Tampa Bay. Clues to their lives and habits of these various tribes can be found in burial practices, initially in wetland cemeteries and then later with circular mounds. Thanks to modern technology and increased awareness of preservation, artifacts and information about the former are being constantly uncovered. Divers recently excavated bodies estimated to be some 8,000 years old in Manasota Key and in another underwater burial site discovered in 2016 in the Gulf of Mexico near Venice.

Sarasota's aboveground burial mounds, however, fared less well, thanks to early 20th-century "pot hunters"—settlers looking for "skeletons, relics and maybe even buried gold," stated Grismer and then, as now, developers who polished off the sites for road and building construction. So while most aboveground mounds are but a dim memory, there are still a few carefully preserved areas, the most impressive being Indian Mound Park in Englewood, about an hour away from Sarasota. Although some bodies have been found there, remnants from the Manasota culture consist of ceremonial and everyday artifacts, including decorative shells and shark teeth, cooking utensils, and arrowheads.

The ancient Timucua were among the first to come in contact with explorers; unpleasant surprises lay ahead.
THEODOR DE BRY'S ENGRAVINGS OF THE TIMUCUA, FLORIDA STATE ARCHIVES

THOSE MEAN SPANIARDS

"The Florida Indians may have had one great, almost fatal fault," wrote Grismer. "They may have bragged about their native land too much during their contacts with the outlanders." Tales of a "land of the greatest riches . . . [including] a fountain whose waters would restore youth!" eventually spread to the Spanish explorers as well as the pirates and treasure hunters who plundered the region in the early to mid-1500s. Initially believed to be an island, "la Florida" was so named by Spanish explorer Juan Ponce de Leon, who first made land in St. Augustine in 1513.

The relatively peaceful natives who didn't flee from the pale-faces and who sailed along and looted Florida's west coast soon became unfriendly. The colorful glass beads and other shiny cheap gewgaws offered by the Spaniards in exchange for wayfinding could only go so far to mitigate the Spaniards' brutality and enslavement practices as well as diseases such as smallpox and measles that they brought with them.

After the Spaniards realized no tangible riches could be found in Florida, they built forts to protect their trade routes and sent peace-loving missionaries into an almost guaranteed 187—police code for homicide. And while some Jesuit groups gained a foothold in other parts of Florida, the one mission in 1549 that landed in Sarasota Bay ended badly. The main priest, Luis de Cancer Barbastro, who had the ironic nickname "Father Cancer," was immediately beaten to death by natives after landing on the beach. The accompanying two priests were captured and likely killed, although "pioneer settlers say they remember seeing the remains of a stone-walled building, which might have been built by the missionaries" close to Sarasota Bay. By 1900, however, any crumbling remnants had completely disappeared. And by the 1700s, the tall, strong Calusa and many other early tribes had also pretty much become extinct.

The most famous explorer credited with "discovering" Sarasota—sort of—was none other than Spanish conquistador

Hernando de Soto. By all accounts, de Soto was a badass, and not in a good way. Along with a well-documented fondness for killing the locals, de Soto, born in 1499, made his bones plundering Guatemala, Yucatan, and Peru, where he conquered the Incas and stripped them of their wealth. He himself became incredibly rich, a multimillionaire by today's standards.

Nevertheless "he wanted still more wealth, more power and a province in the New World he could call his own . . . where he would be the leader who took most of the loot—not a lieutenant who received only a fraction of what the leader got," wrote Grismer. So as a reward for his successful ventures, King Charles V "gave" de Soto governorship of what is now Cuba and Florida. And in November 1538, de Soto took his noble-born bride, Isabella, and nine ships with an army of over 700 men, plus livestock, weapons, foodstuffs, and money, and set sail for Havana.

Leaving Isabella in Havana, he hit the Florida coast the following May. But karma had the last laugh: she never saw him again because he died of fever less than five years later in what is now Louisiana. Having pillaged a good portion of the southern United States and fearing Indian retaliation, his men secretly dumped his body in the Mississippi River in the middle of the night.

According to the *Final Report of the United States: De Soto Expedition Commission*, the closest the expedition actually came to Sarasota was during its first sighting of land on May 26, 1539, at what's now known as Longboat Key. Juan Anasco, an advance scout for explorer Hernando de Soto, sailed to the key in a "long boat," then skedaddled back to the ship after encountering hostile natives.

The expedition then moved on to actually make land in the Tampa Bay area, or some historians argue, Charlotte Harbor (about an hour south of Sarasota) on May 30, 1539. De Soto didn't discover that area either—conquistador Panfilo de Narváez sailed into the Tampa Bay region in late February 1528 with five ships and 400 men.

De Soto "rediscovers" Tampa Bay. Drawing of Hernando de Soto landing at Tampa Bay, 1859.
FLORIDA MEMORY, FLORIDA STATE ARCHIVES

Yet local history has provided de Soto with a lion's share of recognition, despite the fact that he essentially perpetrated the equivalent of a native holocaust. Not only was the first luxury hotel in Sarasota named after him when it was built in 1887, but the 26-acre De Soto National Memorial in nearby Bradenton, with its nature trails, kayak tours, and living history reenactments, offers a modern-day tribute.

At one point, people even believed Sarasota was named after de Soto because, you know, it kind of sounds like it (i.e., "Sara-soto"). In fact, shortly after the Civil War, according to Grismer's account, an imaginative schoolteacher who moved to the region from Ohio perpetrated the frontier version of an urban legend to explain its origins. Other sources, including Sarasota History Alive!, credit George F. Chapline, of Charendon, Arkansas, who visited the area around 1900 and in 1906 and penned the story "The Legend of Sara DeSoto."

Supposedly, Chichi-Okobee, a handsome young Indian prince captured by de Soto's men, caught the eye of de Soto's daughter "Sara," even though there was no record of his having any legitimate children, nor were there any females in his party.

What transpired was the equivalent of a Shakespearian tragedy or at least a novella. First, Chichi-Okobee got what was known back then as Everglades fever, and Sara nursed him back to health; then she fell ill. He asked his powerful medicine man to cure her, but she died anyway. According to this literary equivalent of an eyeroll,

> Broken hearted, Chichi went to De Soto and asked that Sara be buried in Sarasota Bay, the loveliest spot along the sun-kissed shores of Florida. Chichi also begged that he be allowed to take part in the ceremony. De Soto, stricken with grief, gave consent. . . .
>
> The next morning there appeared a hundred Indian braves, headed by Chichi-Okobee. All were bedecked in full war paint; every quiver bristled with stone-tipped arrows; every bow was strung. Three large canoes, draped with the dark mosses of the forest, swept up the beach, paddled by more of Chichi's braves. The body of Sara was tenderly placed in one of the canoes, the funeral barge. In the other two canoes went Chichi and the guard of honor. Slowly the fleet moved to the exact center of Sarasota Bay where Sara's body was lowered gently into the deep. Then, at a signal from Chichi, every warrior sprang to his feet, tomahawk in hand. In strange, weird unison, the hundred braves chanted a funeral dirge. As its mystery-laden echo died away in the depths of the forest along the bay, the blades of a hundred tomahawks crashed into the frail canoes. A moment of ripple. A moment of bubbles. And all was still. Chichi and his companions-at-arms had gone to guard the resting place of the beautiful Spanish maiden in the clear, blue waters of Sarasota Bay. (Grismer, *The Story of Sarasota*, 20)

Oh, please. Regardless of where it came from, this pretty fiction spawned an annual event called the Sara de Soto pageant,

The first king and queen of the annual Sara de Soto Pageant were part of the humble inaugural reenactment in 1916.

which further established the showmanship, artistic flamboyance, and eccentricity that have become Sarasota's trademark. First held in 1916 as a reenactment, by the late 1940s, the festival was the highlight of the late winter tourist season and grew along with the city, evolving into "the most popular festival south of New

Orleans," according to the *Sarasota Herald-Tribune*, a multiday celebration of all things Spanish with a queen and the participation of John Ringling, who, in the 1920s, added the circus touch with an accompanying Orange Blossom festival, "which showcased its performers, clowns, showgirls and exotic animals."

But by 1957 it had run its course, having been replaced a few years earlier with a celebration of Sarasota's Scottish heritage and "which later morphed into the King Neptune Frolics, neither of which matched the spectacle of Sara de Soto," concluded the article.

Sarasota historian John Barth, Jr., offered a more plausible explanation of the name's backstory. "An early Spanish map on sheepskin that turned up in London when Florida passed to British possession in 1763, shows the word 'Zarazote' across present day Bradenton and Sarasota," he wrote in Sarasota History Alive! "When the coast was charted, the name appeared as Boca Sarazota (Sarazota Pass) between Lido and Siesta Keys, and by the 1850s the barrier islands and the bay were both labeled Sarasota on maps."

And as subsequent settlers and the Ringling family itself eventually found out, while a "rose by any other name smells just as sweet," it also has thorns.

Chapter 2

The Early Settlers

OF SEMINOLES AND SLAVES

Much of what happened in Sarasota from the time of the Spanish conquistadors until the early 1800s is either the stuff of legend or found in factual recounting of major players, the majority of whom were wealthy white slave owners. But examining anecdotal glimmers of history, especially with regard to natives, Blacks, and women, might provide insight into what eventually drew an eclectic assortment of robber barons and other innovators—especially the Ringlings—to the area.

EVERYTHING, EVERYWHERE, ALL AT ONCE

Several different events occurred simultaneously or at least within this time period:

The Era of the "Fish Camp"

From the late 1700s until the mid-1800s, Spanish and Cuban fishermen established fish camps (rancheros) on the shores of Sarasota Bay. "Their trade was mainly in mullet and mullet roe, although they also salted drum fish, turtles, and trout to ship south," states Sarasota History Alive! "The Florida Seminole Indian Tribe also frequented the region during this time for hunting, fishing and farming." Some natives eventually ended up working at the rancheros, one of which was located near Whitaker Bayou, a few minutes north of downtown Sarasota. Trendies, hipsters, and the like can sort of re-create that experience today by dining at Owens Fish Camp, which is also downtown.

East and West Florida

At one point, Florida was divided into two sections. It was also subject to frequent changes in ownership, not unlike a used car with a suspicious provenance. "In 1763, France, Britain, and Spain signed the Treaty of Paris at the end of the French and Indian War," according to Exploring Florida. "As part of the treaty, France gave up almost all of its land in North America and Spain gave up Florida. During the French and Indian War, Britain had captured Havana, Spain's busiest port. In exchange for Havana, the Spanish traded Florida to Britain. The British then divided Florida into two territories: East Florida and West Florida." The

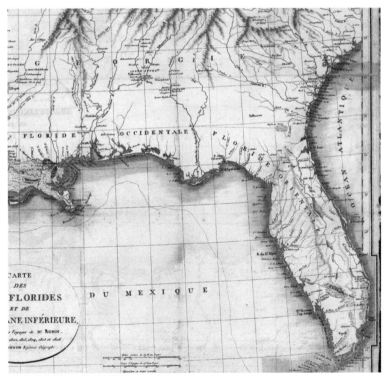

According to this 1807 map, parts of Georgia, Alabama, Mississippi, and Louisiana are actually part of "West Florida." Who knew?
PUBLIC DOMAIN—FLORIDA STATE LIBRARY MAP COLLECTION

Sarasota region and the entire "boot" of what is now Florida was located in East Florida. During the American Revolution, Spain invaded West Florida and by the end of that war had taken over the whole state, so Florida was once again under Spanish rule . . . for a while. In 1821 and after several failed attempts by the Spaniards to colonize, the United States purchased Florida (the whole enchilada) from Spain. "Gaining control of Florida for the United States would mean gaining control of the Mississippi River . . . an important route for trade," explains the site. Florida became a state on March 3, 1845.

The Seminole Wars

Then there were the Seminole Wars—all three of them. "Seminoles came down from Alabama and Georgia in the 1700s, which makes them snowbirds of sorts," writes columnist and author Eliot Kleinberg in the *Sarasota Herald-Tribune*, continuing that:

> [e]ach was ugly, unpopular, and inconclusive. The First Seminole War, in 1818, saw Gen. Andrew Jackson chase Seminoles through northern parts of Spanish Florida, still three years from coming under the Stars and Stripes. The Third Seminole War, a series of skirmishes from 1855 to 1858, was the last Indian war east of the Mississippi. But the most infamous was the Second Seminole War, from 1835 to 1842. It killed 1,500 U.S. soldiers and countless Seminoles. It was the longest and most expensive war the white man ever waged against Native Americans—and draws many parallels to Vietnam. (Eliot Kleinberg, *Sarasota Herald-Tribune*)

In 1840, during the Second Seminole War, Sarasota's first army outpost, Fort Armistead, was constructed. Also located near the Whitaker Bayou/Indian Beach area, it mostly served as a deportation center for Seminoles, who, unless they could escape to the

Everglades, were shunted out west by steamer. At one point there were "nearly 600 troops and an unknown number of civilians and captive Seminoles," according to Sarasota History Alive! Despite efforts to build a hospital and bring in physicians, various fevers and dysentery claimed the lives of the men, so Fort Armistead was abandoned after seven months. And the Seminole Tribe, who never officially surrendered, now manages a half-dozen casinos in Florida. As everyone knows, the house always wins.

It was after the Second Seminole War that South (formerly East) Florida began to open up thanks to the Armed Occupation Act of 1842, a 19th-century guns-not-optional stimulus program:

> This act stipulated that six months' provisions and 160 acres of land, anywhere south of Palatka and Gainesville, would be given to settlers willing to carry arms to defend their homes for five years. And additional land could be bought for $1.25 an acre! (Grismer, *The Story of Sarasota*, 27)

The Arrival of Pioneers, Black and White
Such a deal . . . but even before that, a few intrepid souls began to trickle into the area. Among the first was Josiah Gates. Originally from what is now Tampa, he got wind of the Armed Occupation Act a few months before it was passed and headed toward the scenic and lush Manatee River region with his wife, children, and slaves, putting in his claim so he could establish a hotel to accommodate the anticipated onslaught of homesteaders and explorers. And they did indeed come: among them were "Dr. Joseph Braden, who built Braden Castle on the Braden River; Major Robert Gamble, who built the Gamble Mansion in Ellenton; [and] William H. Whittaker, who would eventually settle in present-day Sarasota," according to *The Bradenton Times*.

All of these pasty-looking men who could have used a few hours on the beach had slaves who were expected to abide by the so-called Florida slave code that also included "free Negroes, and

Although he was a solid citizen, this photo of East Bradenton founder Josiah Gates looks more like a mug shot.

Mulattoes." Enacted in 1828, among many other things, it forbade Black people to read or write and put in place strict rules regarding their congregation and movements. Additionally,

- While Florida law permitted branding, mutilation, and death for some crimes committed by slaves, most masters chose to use a whip to exact punishment.
- A whip that was specifically designed to inflict pain but not leave scars was the choice.
- Whipping kept the slave at work. Punishment by confinement did not. Additionally, a scarred slave might lose value because the scars could brand the slave as a troublemaker.
- Carelessness on the part of slave owners was deemed not in the public good, so slave owners whose slaves had run away and were then later picked up by patrols had serious difficulty ahead.
- Fines of up to $100 could be levied against the owner. Captured runaway slaves were housed in local jails at the owner's expense.
- The patrols that captured the runaway were rewarded, by the owner. Later, the initial $100 fine was jumped to $500, and the runaway could receive 100 lashes.
- For all the controls exercised by whites over Black people, the white settlers seemed to be in constant fear of an insurrection by Black people.
- As a result, selling intoxicants to Black people was a serious crime back in the pioneer days. The punishment for such a deed was a $10 fine or 39 lashes across the back. (Morgan Stinemetz, *Sarasota Herald-Tribune*)

Sarasota's early Black people weren't always in shackles. During Spanish rule, Florida "had been a sanctuary for Black people escaping British slavery," writes Isaac Eger in *Sarasota* magazine.

From 1812 to 1821, what is now Manatee Mineral Springs Park in east Bradenton was the home of Angola, a thriving colony of about 750 "maroons," the colloquial term for escaped slaves. Also called Black Seminoles, they "were descendants of free Black people and runaway slaves, originally from Georgia and the Carolinas, who associated with the Seminoles. Many found refuge with Native American tribes." Angola was "ideal for a community of runaway slaves, [offering] rich soil, a supply of fresh water in the mineral spring and a clear view to the north to spot slave raiders."

In 1821, when Florida's new owners got wind of the community, General Andrew Jackson directed his buddies, the Creek Indians, to attack Angola and burn it to the ground. The surviving inhabitants scattered across Florida and were eventually captured or fled to the Bahamas. And the community itself slipped into almost-obscurity.

DECODING HISTORY

It wasn't until some 170 years later, in 1991, that Newtown native journalist, scholar, and documentarian Vickie Oldham, at the time a graduate student at Florida State University, became intrigued by a mention of Angola in *Florida's Peace River Frontier*, a history of the Seminoles. Newtown is Sarasota's historic community for Black people. Through grants, donations, and a partnership with the New College Public Archaeology Lab, Oldham, along with nonprofit Reflections of Manatee, and a group of amateur volunteers, initiated archeological digs at Manatee Mineral Springs Park. Although they only knew the approximate location of Angola, they used radar tomography to help pinpoint promising sites.

In 2009, they found a single remnant: "buried under three feet and two centuries of earth near the banks of the Manatee River, a cylinder of white clay no bigger than a cigarette butt . . . nearly mistaken for debris and tossed by a volunteer," according to *Sarasota* magazine. It was actually the stem of a British clay pipe and along with other fragments located in subsequent digs, is considered to be among the most significant archeological findings in the State of Florida. Recognized as part of the Underground Railroad Network to Freedom by the National Park Service, the site was also host to the first annual Back to Angola festival in 2018, which featured Bahamian music, wood carving, basket weaving, and food.

Nevertheless, Sarasota's first readily identifiable African American was a slave, Jeffrey Bolding. According to the *Story of Sarasota*, Bolding came to the area in 1857 via North Carolina, escaping a brutal overseer who "forced [Bolding] to work sixteen hours a day in a canebreak . . . and beat him cruelly and often. Jeffrey['s] back . . . was crisscrossed with raw, festering welts, obviously made by a black snake whip."

Bolding was found hidden in a clump of palmettos by William Henry Whitaker, the first recorded settler who had come to the area in the 1840s. Whitaker established himself as a major force there in 1851, where along with his nearly 150 acres of free prime bayfront property courtesy of the federal government, he purchased an additional 48 acres for about $60 (adding at least nine zeros to that amount might begin to touch today's value).

Rather than turning him in, Whitaker, whom history generally regards as a good guy, gave him shelter and eventually ended up buying him from his original owner for the then-exorbitant price of $1,000. Bolding returned the favor through lifelong loyalty, even leaving his wife, Hannah, also a Whitaker slave, to go back to the Whitakers after the couple had been emancipated by the Union Army and sent to Key West. In the late 1860s, he also saved Whitaker's 12-year-old son, Furman, when he accidentally shot himself, by applying a tourniquet to Furman's shattered arm. Bolding remained with the family until his death in 1904, calling himself a "high-priced man" to anyone who would listen and referring to himself as "a thousand-dollar n*****r" to his fellow Black people—shocking in today's context, but revealing much about the mentality of the times.

PIONEERING WOMAN

In 1851, William Whitaker also married Mary Jane Wyatt—the area's first wedding—who in 1852 gave birth to the first white child born in Sarasota, Nancy Catherine Stuart Whitaker, the eldest of their eight children to reach adulthood.

As a young girl, Mary Jane learned how "to ride horseback, herd cattle, paddle a dugout canoe and shoot a rifle, becoming the kind of markswoman who, her father boasted, 'could shoot the head from a wild turkey at 100 yards,'" according to a profile in *Sarasota* magazine. Her soon-to-be husband, William, "had established businesses in cattle, citrus and fishing by the time he dared to ask for Mary Jane's hand."

Along with living through the retaliatory 1856 Seminole raids, including the destruction of her house at the hands of the family's former close friend, Chief Billy Bowlegs—soldiers had humiliated the Indians and destroyed the measly tract of land doled out to them by the government—in 1863, during the Civil War, she also talked marauding Union soldiers out of burning down her just-rebuilt home.

> The men, after ransacking the house of all its belongings not too cumbersome to take along . . . called for matches to set the house on fire. Without arguing, Mrs. Whitaker . . . returned with a block of matches and . . . handed it to the commanding officer and said, "Sir, I want to look into the eyes of a man who can stoop so low as to burn the home of a helpless woman and her family." . . . The soldiers turned away and the house was saved. (Lillie B. McDuffee, *Lures of the Manatee*)

This is but an inkling of what the Whitakers and the other few residents had to endure. While Sarasota was not particularly targeted by the Union troops, "supplies were hard to get due to federal ships patrolling the coastline," states Sarasota History

Four generations of Whitaker family values on display with family crest.
Mary Jane (top right) was one tough customer.
PUBLIC DOMAIN—COURTESY MANATEE COUNTY PUBLIC LIBRARY

Alive! "Union troops would occasionally come ashore to look for supplies and would burn homes and crops. Cattle had to be hidden or it would be taken by the Union troops." As a result, people went hungry and without clothing and other necessities, and William Whitaker "did everything in his power to bring victory to the South," states Grismer in *The Story of Sarasota*. This included donating his cattle to the Confederate Army, running blockades, and operating a hidden grist meal to supply grits and cornmeal to the starving locals. He also made shoes for his own family (think John Ringling cleaning bathrooms because no servants were about).

THE CONFEDERACY: IT'S COMPLICATED

Whitaker was also involved in the escape of what might be referred to today as the notorious JPB, aka Judah P. Benjamin, the so-called "brains of the Confederacy." A plantation owner in New Orleans, Louisiana, and senator and top advisor to Confederate president Jefferson Davis, he was "the first Jew to hold a cabinet-level office in an American government and the only Confederate cabinet member who did not own slaves," according to the Jewish Virtual Library. In 1865, toward the end of the Civil War, with the Union Army hot on his tail, he was smuggled to the mansion formerly owned by Robert Gamble, who had been forced to abandon it and sell his own slaves after the sugar market crashed in the mid-1850s. From there, with an eye to escaping to England via Nassau, Benjamin traveled by horse and buggy to the Whitaker home by the bay, where he boarded a sailboat and slipped away to London, eventually establishing a successful law practice and becoming an advisor to Queen Victoria. Benjamin died in Paris in 1884 at the comparatively ripe old age of 73.

Today, the Judah P. Benjamin Confederate Memorial at Gamble Plantation Historic State Park in nearby Ellenton has the dubious distinction of being South Florida's only antebellum mansion and a monument to the notorious JPB. Rescued from disrepair in the late 1920s by the local Daughters of the Confederacy, it was refurbished and furnished with Civil War and other period items and is available for guided tours and bar mitzvahs (well, maybe not the latter). In 1942, the Daughters of the Confederacy also erected a monument on N. Tamiami Trail, near the spot where Benjamin sailed away. According to Sarasota History Alive!, "The unveiling followed a luncheon at the John Ringling Hotel and a program at the Municipal Auditorium. The program was preceded by a parade in which the participants were nearly 1,000 George Washington Juniors, a patriotic organization of school children."

How times have changed. In July 2020, the monument, along with an accompanying historical marker, was abruptly removed, ostensibly to make way for the construction of a roundabout. As of this writing it is still in storage.

While scholars will debate these events for decades to come, Sarasota faced a different destiny.

Chapter 3

Cow Herders, Assassins, and Lieutenants of Industry

SETTING THE STAGE FOR RINGLING

While Sarasota isn't necessarily associated with cowboys, cattle drives, and vigilantes, the area and Florida in general shared aspects of the Wild West long before Sarasota established its own county on May 14, 1921, breaking away from the larger Manatee County, which had been founded some 66 years earlier, in 1855.

OF COWS AND COWBOYS

Brought over by the Spaniards in the 1500s and left to roam free after they left, cattle played a major role in Manatee County and Florida history. Initially the purview of the Seminoles and Black people and unlike many of the early two-legged settlers, the cattle "were hardy . . . [and] survived on native forage, tolerated severe heat, insect pests, and acquired immunity to many diseases," according to the Historical Society of Sarasota County. This made them far more difficult to locate and round up than their "open range" Western counterparts, especially since they lived in what essentially was a jungle. After being herded into "cow camps," they were driven east by what became known as the Cracker Trail, some 120 miles from Bradenton toward Fort Pierce toward the Atlantic Ocean, where they were shipped to Key West, Nassau, and Cuba.

While often used in the same context as "redneck" or "hillbilly," the term "cracker" is actually derived from the explosion of noise made by 12- to 18-foot-long braided, long-handled buckskin whips

Black cowboy, Archie Rutledge, with fellow herders at Wildes Harrison Ranch in the early 1920s. "Slaves, former slaves and free blacks served important roles as ranch hands, overseers, drovers and independent ranchers in Florida's cattle industry for centuries," Florida Agricultural Museum director Mary K. Herron told NPR.
PUBLIC DOMAIN—COURTESY OF THE MANATEE COUNTY PUBLIC LIBRARY

used by these cow herders. By the mid- to late 1800s, they were mostly working-class white men, although there were some Black people and Natives. The term "cracker" became part of the lexicon of the white, post–Civil War hardscrabble existence in the South, indicative of unpretentious, rustic architecture, music, and lifestyle.

One remaining example of the former is Sarasota's Crocker Memorial Church. Built in 1903 by Civil War veteran Peter Crocker, it was moved several times, refurbished in the 1930s, and purchased by different congregations, even "being rented to various organizations for meetings, music recitals, dances, programs, and . . . many small weddings," in the 1980s, states Sarasota History Alive! In the early 2000s, the City of Sarasota and Historical County of Sarasota relocated the church to Pioneer Park, deeming its wooden frame and simple construction "a perfect example of turn-of-the-century cracker architecture," observes Sarasota's

Boulevard of the Arts website. A few Cracker structures can still be found hidden among the palms and overgrowth in rural and out-of-the-way areas.

Traditionally a point of pride among native Floridians, the Cracker culture seems to have faded into the background. In a rare 1980s interview with local resident Tom "Cracker" Lightfoot, born circa 1892 and a cow herder from ages 12 to 27, he describes various challenges, including traversing foot logs over the swamp to walk several miles to a one-room schoolhouse. "In those days, the parents raised the kids, taught them, laid the law down to them, and they worked," he lamented. "When a boy was five years old, if he was on a farm, he was in the saddle." And everyone, including women, learned how to shoot a gun. While "northern people thought we had them guns . . . to kill people . . . this wasn't so." Rather it was to prevent getting eaten by "five different kinds of panthers . . . black bear, and . . . all other kinds of animals."

Cattle, however, remain proven commodities. Although the last drives along the Cracker Trail took place around 1937 and the fencing laws introduced some 12 years later put an end to the free-range "cow camps," today some 15,000 beef producers bring in almost $550 million annually, according to the Florida Beef Council. Camouflaged among beaches and amusement parks, about 886,000 head of cattle still chew their cuds and expel gas in ranches located primarily in the middle and eastern parts of the state.

BIG-TIME LAND WRESTLING

In 1885, Sarasota made the big time, but not in a way the respectable city fathers would have liked. Rather, it was for the murders of Harrison "Tip" Riley and Charles Abbe carried out by "the notorious Sarasota Assassination Society," of whom "Alfred Bidwell, a former citizen of Buffalo, in good repute . . . is charged with being a member," according to a *New York Times* clipping dated February 2 of that year. And it wasn't until the December 27, 1884, murder of Abbe, the Society's second victim and Sarasota's first postmaster and a prominent citizen, that the local constabulary figured out who was doing these dirty deeds. Among others, the Society also terrorized and threatened Abbe's wife, Charlotte, who herself narrowly escaped being killed.

As with many such situations, politics and land were involved, the politics being that "Abbe was a northerner, a postmaster, a

Although he undoubtedly meant well, Sarasota's first postmaster, Charles E. Abbe, fell victim to the ire of the Sarasota Democratic Vigilante group (not to be confused with today's Democratic Party).
PUBLIC DOMAIN—COURTESY OF THE MANATEE COUNTY PUBLIC LIBRARY

progressive businessman and, worse, a Republican in a mostly Democratic county," states an account in the *Sarasota Herald-Tribune*. Further muddying the waters is the fact that the Democratic Party of the time essentially had what could be considered Republican politics of today and vice versa. In other words, Democrats favored state's rights and slavery as a business model while Republicans supported Abolition (Abraham Lincoln was a Republican), strong federal government, and the rights of working-class people.

Using a loophole in the Homestead Act of 1862, speculators and politicians, knowing that the State of Florida was in debt and that the money and industry from railroads were coming to the area, cooked up a scheme in the early 1880s to deprive many of Sarasota's approximately 60 pioneer families of their land. According to Grismer,

> Many of the pioneers whose lands were deeded to the speculators had not filed homestead claims because they did not know the exact "land map" location of their holdings—they did not know how to describe them as precisely as the law required. Other pioneers, who had been just "squatting," had delayed filing claims because they did not believe there was any need for hurrying. Besides, "claim-jumping" in this region was unknown. Everyone respected the other fellow's rights. (Grismer, *The Story of Sarasota*, 81)

Such shenanigans understandably upset the settlers and equally understandably created tension between the haves and have-nots. And perhaps not quite as easy to relate to, a group of former Confederate soldiers formed the Assassination Society/ Vigilance Committee. "Those who joined, or were forced to join, swore an oath not to reveal anything about the society. The act was punishable by torture and death," stated the *Bradenton Times*, referencing an account in the *Manatee County, Florida Sheriff's Office, 1855-2005, 150th Anniversary History and Pictorial*. "The sole purpose of this committee was to murder five of the area's most prominent men: Robert Greer, Furman Whittaker, Harrison 'Tip' Riley, Charles Abbe and Stephen Goings. . . . In a letter to his parents Pliny Reasoner, a pioneer nurseryman, described them as 'a group of five or six men, a clique of them, who are negro-killers, rascals and yes devils, (I mean it).'"

To this day, however, their precise motive is still up for debate:

When Karl Grismer wrote his "Story of Sarasota" in 1946, he attributed the vigilantes' animosity toward Riley and Abbe to the belief that they assisted speculators who tried to push settlers off the land. Janet Snyder Matthews' later research for "Edge of Wilderness" found no support for that explanation. She concluded that the leaders of the Vigilance Committee operated from personal motives, one of which was jealousy of Abbe's wealth and political power. (*Sarasota Herald-Tribune*)

Bidwell's 1882 home still stands and has been repurposed as the Bidwell-Wood House, the "Wood" portion being the name of the Rhode Island family who purchased the home four years later and finished it to its present level of completion. Moved several times, it was eventually relocated in Pioneer Park near the Crocker church. Also headquarters of the Historical Society of Sarasota, the Bidwell-Wood House stands as one of the few remaining reminders of those rugged years that once again also memorializes the criminal rather than the victim.

During this period, Sarasota also had its share of general lawlessness: "a bunch of cowboys getting lit on sugar cane and riding up and down the street," according to the *Manatee County 150th Anniversary History and Pictorial* as quoted in the *Bradenton Times*. "They shot their pistols in the air from their horses while at full gallop. They yelled obscenities in the middle of the night. Folks were scared to come out of their houses."

FROM SARA SOTA TO SARASOTA

As with many American communities in the late 19th and early 20th centuries, credit for the transformation from an untamed dirt road outback to orderly buildings and streets resembling today's infrastructure was primarily given to wealthy or at least seemingly well-off white men. Sara Sota, as it was called until the 1890s when the U.S. Postal Service set forth guidelines to simplify place names (which included combining two words into one), was no different. The following are among the most recognized originators:

John Webb

"In 1867, John and Eliza Webb and their five children . . . arrived . . . from Utica, New York, claiming 145 acres under the Federal Homestead Act," states Sarasota History Alive! "The Webbs named their homestead 'Spanish Point,' because a Spanish trader in Key West had told them about a high point of land extending out into the bay. Over the next 43 years, three generations of the Webb family cultivated citrus groves, sugar cane, and vegetable crops, built and maintained boats for transportation, and ran the region's first tourist operation known as 'Webb Winter Resort.'"

Arthur (A. B.) Edwards

Born in 1874, Arthur Britton (A. B.) Edwards was not only born in Sarasota, but he made its development his main focus, according to his profile in Sarasota History Alive! "He began this quest when he opened his real estate and insurance office in 1903, on Main Street in downtown Sarasota. Many questioned why a real estate office was needed in a town with only 300 residents, but Edwards knew that the railroad was coming through, which meant potential growth. One problem Edwards had was trying to sell Sarasota to the outside world." Although he didn't have much in the way of capital, "he wrote to the leading railroads throughout the country and asked them to send him the names of people inquiring about Florida." The railroad proved to be a huge game changer for Sarasota.

> In 1903, the U.S. and West Indies Railroad and Steamship Company built a depot. The railroad, subsequently incorporated into the Seaboard Air Line Railway, provided great impetus to the town's turn-of-the-century progress. Trains brought passengers and manufactured goods to Sarasota and took local products such as fish, citrus, lumber, and vegetables to northern markets. The tracks entered the town along Lemon Avenue, crossed Main Street and curved south to terminate on a pier extending into the bay where commercial fish houses were built.
> In 1905 and 1912, tracks were built to the agricultural and commercial centers of Fruitville, Bee Ridge, and Venice. When Ringling Brothers and Barnum and Bailey Circus established winter quarters in Sarasota in 1927, tracks were extended to the circus grounds east of the city. Daily train and sleeper service from Sarasota to points north ultimately succumbed to the convenience of the automobile. The Seaboard Air Line Railway and Atlantic Coast Line Railroad merged in 1967 to form the Seaboard Coast Line which continued train service at its station on east Main Street. (Sarasota History Alive!)

Through newspaper advertisements and personal correspondence, Edwards managed to elicit interest and eventually struck up a friendship with very wealthy Bertha Palmer from Chicago, who became a major force in Sarasota during the 1910s.

HERE COME THE SCOTS, PART I: ALEX BROWNING AND JOHN GILLESPIE

At age 19, "Alex Browning . . . arrived on Sarasota Bay at the end of 1885 with a group of colonists who sailed from Scotland to start a new life in Florida," states his profile on Sarasota History Alive! Persuaded by a pamphlet from the Florida Mortgage and Investment Company, which promised a fully built town, they arrived only to discover it was still a jungle out there and "and soon left for more settled areas. The Brownings remained, however, and quickly became some of the creators of the town." Browning became a certified architect and helped design resilient structures such as the Frances-Carlton Apartments on North Palm Avenue, which are still in use as condos and are listed on the National Register of Historic Places.

John Hamilton Gillespie, the "Father of Sarasota," according to his profile on Sarasota History Alive!, blew into town in 1886 at age 24, where he had been dispatched "to improve the situation" created by the Florida Mortgage and Investment Company, which his father had partial interest in. He remained to organize major thoroughfares, the waterfront, the Episcopal Church, and other enterprises and helped establish many traditionally WASP male bastions of power, including the local Bar Association, the American Legion, Masons, Kiwanis, and more. Not surprisingly, he became Sarasota's first mayor when the town was incorporated in 1902 and served six terms.

But perhaps more importantly, at least for millions of vacationers and retirees, Gillespie was at the forefront of golf. Along with winning several championships, he was considered to be an authority on the sport, introducing what would turn out to be a huge money machine to the great State of Florida. Along with building a nine-hole golf course in Sarasota, he designed several others.

HERE COME THE SCOTS, PART II: OWEN BURNS

If John Gillespie was Sarasota's daddy, Owen Burns was its godfather, "a leader in practically every movement that saw Sarasota grow from a fishing village to one of Florida's leading resort cities," states his 1934 obituary in the *Sarasota Herald-Tribune*. Born of wealth, he came for the tarpon, mullet, bass, snook, and many more species in 1910 and stayed for the land development, that same year purchasing "approximately 75 percent of today's city limits for the negotiated sum of $35,000" from none other than John Gillespie, states author and Burns biographer Jeff LaHurd.

Burns knew a good thing when he saw it, in many senses of the word. Among his accomplishments are the following:

- A lifelong bachelor, Burns married New York socialite Vernona Freeman in 1912, at the ripe old age of 43. She was decades younger and gave him five children, including local historians Lillian Burns and Harriet Burns Stieff. Although he died in 1937, she never remarried, passing away in 1974 at age 80.

- He helped organize the Sarasota Board of Trade—which would later become the Chamber of Commerce—in 1911 and established the first locally owned bank, the Citizens Bank.

- He was responsible for Sarasota's first paved streets as well as the construction of the city's first seawalls, major dredging projects, and the construction of the original causeways that connect downtown Sarasota with St. Armands and Lido Key. He was also instrumental in the push to divide Sarasota from Manatee County.

- During the Florida land boom of the 1920s, Burns oversaw the development of subdivisions such as Golden Gate Point and Sunset Park, and his construction company built circus magnate John Ringling's Ca' d'Zan estate. Burns established several companies to conduct his businesses, including a bank, a construction company, a real estate company, a transportation company, and a dredging company, and paired with John Ringling on several projects. (Partially adapted from *Time-Traveler's Guide, Visit Sarasota*)

Owen Burns: he came for the fishing and stayed to make a killing in land development.
PUBLIC DOMAIN—FROM LILLIAN BURNS COLLECTION. PHOTO COURTESY OF THE SARASOTA COUNTY HISTORY CENTER.

The downtown historic district of Burns Court pays homage to him as does the adjacent Owen's Fish Camp, which seems more of an homage to unpretentious fishing culture with its unfussy Southern-style menu, down-market wooden benches, and paper towel napkins.

TURN OF THE (20TH) CENTURY INFLUENCER

But in true "let's put on a show" circus spirit, Sarasota's most compelling movers, shakers, and heroes come from unexpected places and spectrums of society. Nowhere is that more evident than in Bertha Palmer, "the millionaire matron of Chicago," so labeled by Jessi Smith in "Bertha Palmer: The Woman Who Tamed Wild Sarasota." Palmer's "extraordinary agricultural innovations . . . commitment to horticultural science and livestock-raising methods, and . . . savvy business acumen" are still felt in Sarasota today.

Palmer—according to some sources, her first name was also spelled "Berthe"—was a haute-couture, bejeweled widow who "host[ed] the Chicago World's Fair in 1893 and is often recognized for her connections to European royalty . . . who decorated her Chicago mansion with artwork by Monet, Renoir and Picasso, which she scooped up on shopping sprees in Paris," continues Smith. But like many would-be snowbirds, she got tired of the cold weather and upon reading a *Chicago Sunday Tribune* advertisement for Sarasota placed by A. B. Edwards and realtor J. H. Lord, burst onto the scene in the winter of 1910 "accompanied by her father H. H. Honoré, brother and two sons, Honore and Potter Jr.," states an article in the *Sarasota Herald-Tribune*. "Sarasota, which then had 900 residents (and no electric service), was excited that such a woman was coming to visit. It was also mortified. Surely, they feared, she would not be happy in the Belle Haven Inn." Once the area's best hotel, it was by then noted for its cesspool smells and shabby furnishings. As an alternative, "a portion of the new Halton medical facility was readied as suitable quarters."

But instead of being met with examination tables, uncomfortable chairs, and medical equipment and odors, Palmer and her entourage found themselves ensconced in the quickly redesigned height of luxury, with sparkling décor and furniture. With its beautiful views of Sarasota Bay and large living, sun, and music rooms and multiple bedrooms and indoor baths, the sanitarium was more resort than medical facility. And while patients did

Bertha/Berthe Palmer, a woman ahead of her time, made a huge impact on not only Sarasota but her hometown of Chicago as well.
PUBLIC DOMAIN—COURTESY OF THE SARASOTA COUNTY HISTORY CENTER

receive care, "many went fishing and brought back big catches," notes Karl Grismer in *The Story of Sarasota*. Not surprisingly, it was run by physician Jack Halton "the singing doctor," a British transplant who had previously practiced medicine in Cincinnati and Muncie, Indiana, also noted for his baritone performances at the Metropolitan Opera in New York and Philadelphia Philharmonic Symphony. Only in Sarasota!

How Palmer actually got to Sarasota, however, may be a point in question. Many accounts state she rode by a train that went as far as Fruitville Road, although according to Grismer, she arrived by a private car, presumably a motor car. Regardless, the locals' efforts paid off. "Once [Palmer] arrived . . . and commented that the isolated and impoverished town was 'refreshingly quaint,' Sarasotans realized they had worried for nothing," states the *Sarasota Herald-Tribune*. "Bertha Palmer was as comfortable with common people as with kings." Along with purchasing almost 90,000 acres "about a quarter of the land in what was to become, in 1921, Sarasota County . . . she also bought in Hillsborough County, owning 140,000 Florida acres at one time," continues the *Herald-Tribune* article.

"What makes Palmer's contributions particularly extraordinary is the age at which she first set to work on them—during the sixth and final decade of her life—and in an era when women's rights were limited," stated Smith in her account. This included the right to vote, which was not ratified until 1920, two years after her death in 1918 at age 69.

"Late in life, when she had money galore, there was really no need for her to do anything, and yet this was a woman who was very bright and who excelled at everything she turned her hand to," observed Frank Cassell, author of *Suncoast Empire: Bertha Honore Palmer, Her Family, and the Rise of Sarasota, 1910-1982*. "She played golf, she fished, and she loved to motor at a time when motoring was a sport. She went to Europe before World War I, and she drove all over the place. She had speed boats. She was extraordinarily social. She threw great parties at Spanish Point for her neighbors and local young people." Palmer worked just as hard and accomplished even more.

From Swamp Things to Profitable Farms
"The agricultural subdivision Palmer created at Bee Ridge was one of the earliest of its kind in the United States," continues Smith in her article. "She transformed the 10,000-acre region by building a

canal system to drain its marshes, and on the newly-drained land, she created ten and 20-acre farms which were honeycombed by smaller canals."

"Beefing" Up Cattle Production

"Prior to Palmer's science-based intervention . . . [in which she] implemented livestock raising practices that adhered to USDA research . . . the cracker ranching style permitted cattle to roam free, leaving them susceptible to parasites that thrive in the subtropical Florida wilderness," observed Smith.

This included the Texas fever tick, which she helped eradicate by building concrete dipping vats and bathing her cattle in an arsenic and soda solution, according to Sarasota History Alive! Although she was initially criticized for this and other innovations, "the *Sarasota Times* called the first dipping in November 1915 'more important in the history of Manatee County than any other corner-stone laying or other imposing ceremonial.'"

Trains and Automobiles

At the time of Palmer's arrival, most roads in the area were "little more than sandy paths overgrown with scrub—better suited for a mule team than a Ford Model T," stated Smith. Recognizing that good transportation made for good business, "Palmer leveraged her wealth, business acumen, and social influence to build railroads as far south as modern-day Venice . . . advocate[ing] the development of local roadways that provided early automotive access throughout the region—and would ultimately define county lines between Manatee and up-and-coming Sarasota."

But perhaps people today most associate Palmer with what is now Myakka River State Park, part of which 58 acres encompass her ranch, Meadowsweet Pastures. Although the brainchild of A. B. Edwards, it wasn't until after the Great Depression that it became a reality, thanks to the State of Florida's foreclosure on more than 6,000 acres in the Myakka lower lake region in 1934 and Edwards's connections with trustees of the Palmer estate, from whom he purchased more than 17,000 acres, 1,900 of which Bertha's sons, Honore and Potter, donated in her memory. Opened in 1942, it has expanded since then.

Along with providing a showcase for the Myakka River, "Florida's first state-designated wild and scenic river . . . flow[ing] through a vast expanse of unspoiled wetlands, prairies, hammocks, and pinelands," according to the Florida State Parks website, the park offers hiking, biking, kayaking, and more amid "the cries of limpkins and osprey . . . while alligators and turtles sun lazily on logs and riverbanks." Through her agriculture and other efforts, forward-thinker Bertha Palmer helped lay the groundwork for Sarasota's appeal for, among many others, John Ringling and his family.

THE BLACK EXPERIENCE: OVERTOWN/ NEWTOWN AND THE KKK CIRCUS

Black people also played a major role in Sarasota's development, although they were hardly as high profile and venerated as their white counterparts. "Black labor cleared snake infested land for real estate developers, laid railroad ties, harvested celery, helped plat golf courses and labored in the homes of Sarasota's influential power brokers cooking, cleaning, ironing and rearing children," stated Rosalyn Howard, PhD, and Vickie Oldham, MFA, in *Newtown Alive: Courage, Dignity, Determination.* Among the post–Civil War standouts are the following:

Reverend Lewis Colson

According to *Newtown Alive,* the first freed former slave to settle in Sarasota after the Civil War was Colson, who arrived in 1884. By 1885, he was gainfully employed with the Florida Mortgage and Investment Company, surveyors who laid out the city of Sarasota, and became a landowner himself. Colson's wife, Irene, was a midwife who birthed babies at home. "Due to Jim Crow laws [Blacks] were unable to obtain most medical services," states the

Lewis Colson and his wife, Irene, were pioneers in establishing
Sarasota's Black community at the turn of the 20th century.
PUBLIC DOMAIN—COURTESY OF THE SARASOTA COUNTY HISTORY CENTER

book. The Colsons were instrumental in establishing the Bethlehem Baptist Church, Sarasota's first Black church, in selling it in 1897 to its trustees for $1, a bargain even back then. He also served as its minister from 1899–1915. He and Irene also have the dubious honor of being the only Black people buried in the all-white Rosemary Cemetery, sharing grave space with the likes of Gillespie, Browning, and Burns, along with other paleface pioneers.

Leonard Reid

An educated man—a rarity in those days—and class valedictorian at Savannah Normal School, Reid came to Sarasota in 1900. He worked for a local fish merchant, then was hired as a manservant to John Hamilton Gillespie, marrying Eddye Coleman, who was also employed by Gillespie as a maid and a cook. The two men had a mutually beneficial relationship—Gillespie advised Reid on successful land purchases, and "Reid assisted Gillespie in laying out the design for Sarasota's first golf course and served as the first greens keeper," states *Newtown Alive*. Along with others, Reid and his wife also founded the Payne Chapel African Methodist Episcopal (AME) Church, Sarasota's second Black church, in 1903.

According to historian Jeff LaHurd, author of *Sarasota—A History*, "Writer Richard Glendinning wrote of [Reid], 'he carried himself with the dignity of a Scottish chieftain.'" Reid's 1952 passing was also noted in the local papers as "Pioneer Negro Citizen Dies," compliments deemed questionable without the narrow telescope of segregation.

Emma Booker

Although her name graces Newtown's elementary, middle, and high schools and Booker Avenue in Sarasota is named after her, only recently has she gotten some press.

"[A] pioneering educator of her time, [she] began teaching while still in her teens herself. Born in Live Oak, Florida, she moved to segregated Sarasota around 1914 to teach at Sarasota's only public school for Blacks, then called Sarasota Grammar. . . . Classes for Black students then were held in rented buildings, with often inadequate and secondhand books and supplies. But Booker was determined to do better. By 1923, she had become the principal of Sarasota Grammar and headed a fund-raising drive to open the community's own school building in 1925, with four classrooms and an auditorium. . . . There she expanded the programs each year until she had eighth-grade graduates. Eventually, as the boom of the 1920s was replaced by the Depression, and her request to add a ninth-grade class was denied by the school board, Booker left Sarasota to take a position in St. Petersburg's school system. . . . But her influence here was undeniable, not only in the schools that bear her name but in those early students—many of whom became educators themselves—she personally helped to see a path forward in a time and place where the odds were stacked against them. (*Sarasota* magazine)

For 20 years, during her summers off, Booker also attended college, finally getting her bachelor's degree in 1937, two years before her death.

A HISTORY CHARGED WITH TENSION

Initially Sarasota's small but thriving Black community settled in a 20-acre district close to Downtown Sarasota. Called "Black Bottom" (for obvious reasons) and then "Overtown," slang of that time period meaning close to downtown, by the 1920s, the population had increased greatly as Sarasota began to grow. "African-American[s] owned restaurants, cafés, clubs and a movie theatre" states the *Bradenton Times*. "Because of Jim Crow laws, residents were not allowed to shop at white-owned stores, so out of necessity, black businesses began popping up. A fish market, grocery store, blacksmith and many other businesses also offered goods and services to black residents. There was even a baseball park." As happened in Harlem and elsewhere in the United States, there was also a burgeoning jazz scene, although many of the big names avoided the area due to "lack of accommodations." It wasn't until 1926 that the first "Negro" hotel opened, called the Colson Hotel, named after Lewis Colson but not owned by him.

Development for "Newtown" Sarasota's most well-known historical Black community "began in earnest in 1914 by Charles Thompson, a . . . circus manager who desired to make the quality of life better for Sarasota's African-American community," observed *Newtown Alive*. A white man, Thompson was a close associate of the Ringlings and according to LaHurd, Newtown's initial 40 acres had 240 lots purchased "on easy payments" and was "exclusive for colored people."

While "the cement block houses of Newtown were a real step up from the dilapidated wooden structures . . . in Overtown," continues *Newtown Alive*, and "houses were nicer and there was lots of open space for children to play," the reasons behind its establishment weren't necessarily altruistic:

> Overtown's proximity to Rosemary Cemetery became a concern for white Sarasotans, who considered moving the cemetery as "the location, having to pass through the colored quarters to reach the cemetery is not desirable." The blacks were encouraged to move further north. (LaHurd, *Sarasota: A History*)

"The Roaring '20s were among the hardest times for Sarasota's African American community," continues LaHurd.

> These were the days when it was not unusual for authorities to "round up" African American men, charge them with "idleness" and order them to pay a fine. Since they

often could not pay, they would be placed on the chain gang. One story in the *Sarasota Herald* was headlined, "Doing Nothing But It Costs. Sarasota Negroes Find They are Not Lillies of the Field." The story related how twenty-nine black men were rounded up in a poolroom, charged with "idleness" and fined twenty-five dollars each, plus court costs. The arrests were made because the sheriff had received numerous complaints that it was impossible to find labor. Another story, "Judge Hard on Negro Idlers" noted that "every Negro seen loafing on the street was questioned." (LaHurd, *Sarasota: A History*)

But just as and if not more frightening and horrifying was "Sarasota's branch of the Knights of the Ku Klux Klan, the Invisible Empire . . . Klan Number 72," continues LaHurd. "The Ku Klux Klan was often a visible presence here, with cross burnings and other forms of intimidation, both physical and psychological."

On October 18–23, 1926, when the "Bob Morton Circus" under the auspices of the KKK, came to town, Ringling was well established as a major player in the industry, further shoring up the guise of legitimacy. "The circus had been staged to raise funds to build a Klavern (Klan headquarters), which would 'exceed anything of its kind south of Atlanta,'" added LaHurd.

Along with "100 big circus stars" and "30 sensational acts," according to the circus's promotional flyer, among the other things these clowns touted were "See popular young local couple get married at the circus tent." One can only imagine the family stories handed down about that particular nuptial. ("The guy in the white hood? Oh, he's just the best man. . . . Everyone wore those back then.")

"The fact that the Klan circus was so well received underscored the sentiment of the times," continues LaHurd. "In conjunction with the circus, 354 men and 82 women, local Klan members, marched down Main Street in their white Klan outfits, watched

Creepy clowns in white hoods dominated the Klan circuses, which toured Florida and the South.
PUBLIC DOMAIN—FLORIDA MEMORY—FLORIDA STATE ARCHIVES

by thousands. . . . The parade was preceded by two fiery crosses . . . with the flag carried by the women members of the Klan auxiliary."

While an ugly mark on Sarasota and circus history, burning crosses and terrorizing minorities were likely the last thing John and Mable Ringling had on their minds when they visited Sarasota for the first time in 1909.

RING TWO
The Family Circus

Chapter 4

Let's Put on a Circus

A QUINTET (ACTUALLY, SEPTET) OF TEUTONIC TROOPERS

By their very nature, circuses are rife with legends, misinformation, and rumors. But the Ringling family—and particularly John Ringling and his older brother, Charles—stands stilts and shoulders above the shills, con men and women, and outlandish freakishness that can comprise its sometimes less than savory underbelly. By nearly all accounts, the Ringling family brought unprecedented credibility and some degree of honesty to an often ruthless and cutthroat enterprise.

EARLY DAYS WITH THE BROS

What started out as a band of brothers putting on a literal dog and pony show (with cats, rabbits, and poultry thrown in) in a barn in McGregor, Iowa, in front of their schoolmates in the 1870s is in many ways similar to Steve Jobs, Steve Wozniak, and Ronald Wayne creating the first Apple computer around 100 years later in Jobs's parents' garage. In 1847, the brothers' father, August Rüngeling, emigrated to Canada from either the Alsace region in northeastern France or Hanover, Germany, depending on the historical account. Regardless "the Ringlings have always considered themselves of German descent," notes August's son Alfred in *The Life Story of the Ringlings*, claiming a proud military heritage and affiliation with the "Fatherland," although it should be noted that his book was initially published in 1900, well before the onset of two world wars.

August worked his way across the country, eventually landing in Milwaukee, where either in 1850 or 1852—again, accounts
vary—he met and married one Marie Salóme Juliar, who lived
on the family farm with her three sisters and brother. At some
point August also changed his name to the more American-
ized *Ringling*. The newlyweds moved to Chicago where August
found employment at a wagon factory with his brother-in-law,
a man named Gottlieb Gollmar, whose wife, Marie Magdalene,
was Marie Salóme's sister. Marie Magdalene bore four sons, who
started their own circus a few years after the Ringlings, eventually
buying their wagons after they (the Ringlings) converted to railroad transportation and even more eventually going to work for
them when they (Gollmar Bros.) closed their own circus in 1916.
Are we there yet?

Not quite. . . . August and Marie Salóme had seven sons and
one daughter, the years of which also differ depending on the
source. According to Ancestry.com and records from the Ringling
Museum archives, they are as follows: Albrecht (called Albert or
Al) born on December 13, 1852 (Chicago); August Albert (called
Gus) on July 20, 1854 (Milwaukee); William Henry (Otto),
June 28, 1858 (Baraboo, Wisconsin); and the rest of the boys in
McGregor, Iowa—Alfred Theodore (Alf T.) on November 16,
1861; Carl Edward (Charles) January 19, 1864; John Nicholas,
May 31, 1866; and Henry William George, October 27, 1868.
The youngest and only girl, Ida Loraina Wilhelmina Ringling, was
born on February 21, 1874, in Prairie du Chien, Wisconsin.

Although his primary occupation was that of a self-employed
harness maker, August was in many ways a jack-of-all-trades, taking whatever jobs were related to his skills and relocating wherever
the work was to support his growing family while at the same time
creating a basis for the comfortable itinerancy that is the foundation of circus life. Although he first moved to Baraboo, Wisconsin,
in 1855, again following the Gollmars, "he immediately established what he called 'A One-Horse Harness Shop,'" according to

Are We There Yet? Second Gen: Two Henrys and a John

While the Ringling penchant for using the same names—including marrying people with the same names—can be confusing, it also provides a glimpse into the second generation's dedication to preserving the continued success of the family circus. Along with serving as the circus's owner and manager until it was sold to the Feld family in 1967 for $8 million, Ida's Ringling son, Henry Ringling North (1909–1993) was a decorated World War II veteran and author of *The Circus Kings*, considered to be a definitive family memoir. His older brother, John Ringling North (1903–1985), the circus's president and director, inherited his namesake uncle's managerial skills in bringing the flailing Big Top into the 20th century, including a switchover from trains to trucks. John R. North also played a part in the 1952 biopic, "The Greatest Show on Earth."

The second generation of Ringlings also spawned another Henry, Henry Ellsworth Ringling (1906–1955). Known as "Little Henry," although he grew to be 6 feet 2 inches and weighed well over 200 pounds, he was a "good-natured fellow whose mother had deliberately alienated him from circus life," according to Henry Ringling North, for reasons not mentioned. Little Henry was still involved with the family business though, managing the Al Ringling Theatre in Baraboo and helping to stage an annual children's show there. He and his son, the not surprisingly monikered Henry Jr., both had somewhat mysterious deaths: Henry Sr. at age 49 in Sauk County, Wisconsin, in 1918 from causes unknown and Henry Jr. in 1962 at age 23, when he smashed his sports car by missing an off-ramp in Baraboo.

Here's where it really gets fun. Along with being married in 1902, both sets of second-generation parents were named Ida and Henry. In the case of John and Henry Ringling, it was the sister, Ida, who was the mother—she married Harry Whitestone North (1858–1921), almost 20 years her senior. With (not so) Little Henry, Henry Ringling was the father, who wed Ida Belle Palmer (1868–1966), also of Baraboo.

Jerry Apps in *Ringlingville, USA*. A clever wordplay on "one-trick pony," August also revealed the roots of his sons' showmanship by claiming of the various bridles, whips, brushes, and more that he had in stock that "there is danger of them being gone in a short time," along with praising their cheap cost and limited availability.

August did well until the Panic of 1857, when he sold all his belongings in hard-hit Wisconsin and moved to McGregor, Iowa, about a year later, "where the need for harness makers was great," according to Apps's book. August opened another shop, closed it again during the Civil War when he went to work for another harness maker, then reopened it again in 1867. He stayed within sight of his adopted state—McGregor is located across the river from Prairie du Chien, Wisconsin, where the family moved in 1872, once again to escape hard times. Two years later, they relocated to Minnesota, where they remained for a brief period, and then it was back to Baraboo, where they stayed in the general area. And yes, we are finally there.

As they were growing up, his sons, particularly the oldest two, Al and Gus, helped in various ways and learned the harness-making trade, skills that would also prove useful in not only dealing with all kinds of customers and vendors but also in the setting up and tearing down of tents and other apparatus and handling of animals that are the backbone of circus life.

"While the family did have modest beginnings and the usual ups and downs as fortunes fluctuated, none of the children ever missed a meal or lived in any degree of poverty," observed Gene Plowden in *Those Amazing Ringlings and Their Circus*.

Again, other accounts disagree. Although they may have appeared to do well enough in McGregor, owning land and businesses, they were mortgaged to the hilt, living in a house in what was then called Walton Hollow from 1859 to 1872. Now privately owned, the "Ringling House" was a local attraction until it was damaged in a fire in December 2021; as of this writing, its fate is unknown.

From humble seeds do great things grow. The Ringling brothers' child-
hood home.
THE JOHN AND MABLE RINGLING MUSEUM OF ART ARCHIVES, PAPERS OF JOHN RING-
LING, COLLECTION OF RINGLING FAMILY PHOTOGRAPHIC ALBUMS

According to longtime McGregor resident Gretchen
Daubenberger,

> The town's practical nurse and midwife came to see her
> mother who was baking bread. "Mrs. Daubenberger," she
> exclaimed, "the Ringlings up the Hollow have just had
> another baby. There isn't a second sheet for the mother's
> bed, nor a stitch of clothing for the new babe. It is a pitiful
> state of affairs."
>
> "My mother was ever generous to a fault," Miss
> Daubenberger reminisces, and so, when the nurse left,
> "she took with her a generous roll of baby clothes we chil-
> dren had all worn, fresh bed linen and most of the morn-
> ing's baking for the Ringling family and . . . set to work
> to 'sponge down' another batch of bread." (*Palimpsest*, a
> publication of the State Historical Society of Iowa)

"Living in such dire poverty no doubt had a great influence on the Ringling Brothers later in life," noted Apps.

When it comes to instilling the stubbornness and resilience that resulted in the Ringlings' eventual domination of the circus world, the retellings seem to converge somewhat. "August and Marie Salomé, both grave in manner and anxious for their children's good, lived out their thoroughly puritan precepts of unfailing honesty, self-discipline and fidelity," observed David C. Weeks in *Ringling, The Florida Years, 1911-1936.* "They provided a homely example of the Teutonic work ethic. August doggedly refused to give up the harness maker's craft even as he watched the market's continual decline, and Marie Salomé kept their home and family standards with a rigor equal to her husband's."

LET'S PUT ON A SHOW . . . FOR THE REST OF OUR LIVES

While their foundation was solid, it also did nothing to hamper the boys' fascination and passion for the circus, understandably typical among children and even adults in an era when the main form of entertainment was going to church, drinking, and taking care of farm animals and crops. In the 1860s, "circuses traveled mostly by horse-drawn wagons, a few traveled by rail and several traveled by steamboat on the Ohio and Mississippi Rivers," noted Apps. Their presence no doubt generated the same kind of excitement as half-time entertainment and/or ads during the Super Bowl and depending on who's playing, possibly even the teams.

And it was here that a few years after the Civil War—again, historians disagree on the date and even the circus itself—a "great day" dawned "in the lives of these boys, who for two weeks had read and reread the crude posters on the walls of McGregor, which announced that on this particular morning a circus was coming to town . . . a boat show which announced its approach by glaring rosin torches and a river calliope," wrote Alf Ringling, conjuring up mental images of Tom Sawyer and Huckleberry Finn, whose creator Samuel Clemens was a distant relative by marriage to the Ringlings and who "lived in a similar river town, called Hannibal, Missouri," noted John's nephew, Henry Ringling North in *The Circus Kings: Our Ringling Family Story.*

According to Alf Ringling, this fortuitous event took place in 1870 with Dan "The King of American Clowns" Rice's circus. "[Rice] was beloved by the crowds and was a friend of the great," noted Ringling North. "Though there was only one ring, it was an excellent show. Indeed, it is thought to be the one Tom Sawyer saw," referring to Clemens's famous fictional character. At one point, Rice even contemplated running for president, underscoring the idea of a clown as chief executive as hardly new.

Although John Ringling was a toddler during this time and Charles only a few years older, they were undoubtedly influenced by their older brothers, especially Al, whose idea it was to form this particular family circus in the first place.

Feeding meat to the lions during the Ringling boys' childhood is today's equivalent of getting the hottest ticket on Broadway or to a rock concert.
LIBRARY OF CONGRESS

Their mother, Marie Salóme, encouraged the boys' musical talents by teaching them various instruments and songs. As a result, according to Plowden, "soon there was an orchestra in the family." They "formed a singing group, clowned and told stories as they entertained at church suppers and socials," with Charles on the violin and trombone and Alf on the cornet.

Even though he still worked for his father, "Al was becoming quite proficient as a balancer and juggler," continued Plowden. "He went to work on the horizontal bars and trapeze and practiced every spare moment." Al even learned to walk the tightrope by stretching a rope between two trees and making his own balancing pole. His brothers followed suit, eventually freaking out the locals, "who were certain they would kill themselves," noted Apps when they walked on wires between two hotels in what passed for downtown McGregor, from which they emerged "unscathed and smiling." Who needs farm animals for entertainment when you have the Ringlings?

"The Ringling boys began putting on their own 'circuses' on Saturdays," Apps went on. The boys went to school and learned to read and write, achieving varying degrees of education while at the same time creating a base for their initial audience of children who were willing to pay a whopping sum of 10 straight pins (and later a penny) for the thrill of seeing "a parade down Main Street . . . over to a barn . . . with an outside animal show before the performance." Along with aforementioned dogs, kittens, and roosters, other attractions included a huge bullfrog "'captured at great risk from the depths of a far-away swamp from which no other frog-collector ever emerged alive,' and Mrs. Ringling's canary 'the head of a great dynasty.' The boys performed on swings and walked across a long beam."

But it was the family's zigzagging fortunes that likely forged their desire to strike out on their own; had circumstances been different, they might have ended up as bankers or shop owners. "Show business couldn't be any harder than harness making, or so it seemed to Al, John, Alf T., and Charles as they considered start-ing a traveling hall show or organizing a circus," stated Apps. A precursor to vaudeville, hall shows were held indoors with a variety of singing and dancing acts, and some of them were quite bawdy, although the Ringlings drew the line at skimpy costumes.

And while multitalented and skilled, each of the brothers had brought his own particular flavor to what would become "The Greatest Show on Earth." Although P. T. Barnum initially coined the phrase, it was also used when Barnum & Bailey merged with Ringling. While none of the other brothers had professional experience, Al and Alf T. had worked with other tent shows before enlisting Otto, Charles, and John to form their own, circa 1882. Again, accounts vary as to when Gus and Henry jumped aboard that particular enterprise, but according to www.wisconsin history.org, it was in 1884, around the time the Ringlings officially launched their first show on May 19 of that year.

THE FIVE FINGERS OF RINGLING

Although on the surface, the brothers may have "seemed as alike as seven Siamese twins," notes Ringling North, each of the five partner brothers had a distinct role, which was cast fairly early on.

With his variety of skills and as the oldest, **Al** was the natural leader, especially in the beginning. A "true performer," he was also the ringmaster "and held the post for life," stated Weeks. His repu-tation among circus people was that of a man who was "modest, unassuming, affable, and courteous," according to *Billboard* maga-zine. Added Weeks, "His wife, Louise, was a skilled equestrian, the only performer among the Ringling wives; she also helped out as a snake charmer in the side show, made costumes, and filled a dozen needs on the lot. One of Al's strategies to make the show seem larger was to have performers change costume and reappear in another ring, creating the illusion of a much larger troupe."

Alf T. acted as the producer. "His artistic ability made the Ringling show well and favorably known and his productions were the most lavish ever seen in the tented arena," observed Plowden. Along with writing and choreographing music and dance numbers, "which filled all three rings and intervening stages . . . with horses, dogs, doves and pretty girls on a swing, pedestals and revolving stage [and] with as many as 1,200" cast members, Alf T. "designed and executed magnificent displays which were a feature of the Ringling Brothers Circus for more than thirty years." A perfectionist who extensively researched and rewrote offerings for each new season, he often spent "days and weeks in museums to find authentic costumes and background material." **Charles**:

> began as the circus's orchestra leader and violinist. Like his brothers, he had a flair for self-taught skills—playing a variety of band instruments in the winter hall shows. Through the big show years, even when the circus had a full professional band, he continued to play at least once each season from a seat among the musicians. His life-long management role was to be the administrator of the whole crew—performers and work force alike. For this he was well suited; he could manage the tumult of circus life, yet he was always "Mr. Charlie" to the whole organization, a name suggesting their respect and affection. (Weeks, *Ringling: The Florida Years*, 27)

Charles remained an equally important influence in the family circus, serving as a guiding managerial force until his death in 1926. Along with John and Mable, he and his wife, Edith, were a major power couple in Sarasota and elsewhere.

The most frugal and almost puritanical in his lifestyle—especially compared to his flamboyant, gregarious brothers—**Otto** handled the money and was the least-liked among workers, of whom he was chronically suspicious and sometimes referred to him as "King Otto." "A master of logistics and arithmetic . . .

[Otto] kept a sharp and distasteful eye on everyone connected with the circus, and attacked waste and inefficiency wherever he found it," stated Plowden. Yet without his corner cutting and stinginess, the show would likely not have gone on, especially during the early years.

While able to hold his own in terms of singing, dancing, and entertaining, **John**, the youngest of the initial five, dropped out of high school (again) at age 16 to join his brothers after they'd been on the road for a few months, much to his parents' great displeasure. Even at a young age, handsome, charismatic John was a bit of a hell-raiser:

> boiling with that tremendous energy which later made him the most far-ranging of the brothers, both in business and intellectual activities. When he was twelve years old [he] struck out for himself. He ran away from home and set himself up in business in Milwaukee. When the police, whom Grandfather had alerted, caught up with John, they found him living in an empty warehouse in Milwaukee, industriously mixing up a batch of Ringling Cleanser. But business was booming. He was very annoyed at being sent home. In the next two years John ran away three more times. (Ringling North, *The Circus Kings*, 50)

Although initially a comedian/clown—among other entertainments, his stage debut included a wooden-shoe dance—he also evolved into a wheeler and dealer, gaining steam and cunning as the years advanced. Unlike "Mr. Charlie," John was generally referred to as "Mr. Ringling" in later years and regarded by employees as mostly diffident and aloof and living in a cultural and economic stratosphere completely different from their own.

Thus, a fortune began to be made. And while essentially ethical, at times the brothers could also be ruthless and conniving, "form[ing] a powerful fist that could drive their opposition to

The Rising Young Dutch Comedian.

It's not only the Internet that lives forever. This postcard of John as a Dutch clown would come back to haunt him as he gained wealth and fame.
THE JOHN AND MABLE RINGLING MUSEUM OF ART ARCHIVES COLLECTION OF POSTCARDS

the wall . . . or grasp it like an octopus and strangle it," observed Plowden.

WAGONS, ROLL!

By 1882, Al Ringling was organizing his brothers and launching their first undertaking, the alliterative "Ringling Brothers Classic and Comic Concert Company." Especially during those days, when folk had no compunction about throwing eggs as well as other organic and nonorganic objects at performers and/or riding them out of town with brandished shotguns, this was risky business. "Preachers commonly railed about actors and their loose morals and . . . performances [being] motivated by the devil himself," Apps went on. The cash-strapped Ringlings faced a daunting profit potential. Making a living in the hardscrabble, still-rugged Midwest was mostly a struggle for their target audience of rural and small-town folks who had little if any disposable income. Still, demographics were in the Ringlings' favor; by 1900, the number of people in Wisconsin alone had increased by almost two-thirds, from about 1.31 million to 2.07 million.

Their first performance on November 27, 1882, was in Mazomanie, Wisconsin, about 25 miles away, far enough so that no one from Baraboo would recognize them should they flop. Observed Alf T., "We had about a thirteen-dollar house, but the fifty-nine people composing the audience looked bigger to me than an audience of fifteen thousand under our tents does today. It seemed as if every individual knew our history, and was aware that this was our first attempt, if not perhaps our first offense, and was ready to guy [mock] and laugh at our efforts."

The troupe included the following:

Al Ringling (plate spinner, juggler), Alf T. Ringling (leader of the band), Charles Ringling (leader of the orchestra), E. M. Kimball (. . . Comedian), E. S. Weatherby (tuba and double bass), Fred Hart (song and dance), and Wm. Trinkhouse (song and dance, alto player, Indian club). M. A. Young was the advance agent. (Plowden, *Those Amazing Ringlings*, 30)

Although the brothers lost money during that first show, they learned as they went along, stopping at every Podunk burg in their known universe. Although exhausted from lack of sleep and uncomfortable conditions, they gained audiences and experience, along with respectability and reasonable profit, and traveled by any means available from farm drays and hired wagons to trains and staying at fleabag (or worse) lodgings, rarely if ever losing sight of the "biz" in "show biz." In 1884 when they added the word "Circus," to their enterprise, they were already experienced troopers who had quite a few bumps along the way. This included ditching an entire cast of drunken and disorderly performers in Minnesota during the bitterly cold winter of 1883—they paid them, as they paid all their bills, even if they had to abscond during the night and send money later.

In the spring of 1884, they enlisted some help:

Al Ringling had worked for Fayette Lodawick "Yankee" Robinson during the summer of 1883, and he convinced the white-whiskered circus veteran (then sixty-six) to join the Brothers in forming their first circus. One of the best-known circus showmen in the country, Robinson helped Al design a ninety-minute program and helped plan a wagon route for the circus that would start in Baraboo, stop in several Wisconsin towns, then move into Iowa and Minnesota, Illinois, and back to Wisconsin. Recognizing Robinson's drawing power, the Boys named the show "Yankee Robinson and Ringling Bros. Great Double Shows, Circus and Caravan." It was the only time the Ringlings put someone else's name ahead of theirs in billing a show. (Apps, *Ringlingville, USA*, 18)

Considered ancient by 19th-century standards, Robinson intended to "die in harness"—his words—and intuited "that the Ringling brothers are the future showmen of America." He was right on both counts, passing away unexpectedly while en route to visit his son on September 4, 1884, less than four months after the circus's debut. While this was a setback and after finishing out their commitments for the rest of the month, the brothers returned to their "Carnival of Fun" for part of the following year. Without the heft of Robinson's name and experience and without an elephant, which was considered de rigueur for circuses of the day, the small but efficient collection of horses, tents, colorful costumes, and Ringlings known in that era's vernacular as "contortionists, balancers, jugglers and comedy acts" weren't quite there yet. Not then, anyway.

Chapter 5

Hitting the Big Time with the Big Top

In mid-1885, John Ringling had a brainstorm. "I ought to go ahead, scoutin' for the best stands [stops]," John allegedly told his brothers, according to Gene Plowden's *Those Amazing Ringlings and Their Circus*. "It can mean real cash for us. A good front man ought to keep his eyes open and ears tuned so he knows where to put the show to make money; where there's a celebration we might tie in with; or [whether] we ought to pass up the town entirely."

Showing marketing acuity and maturity ahead of the times and his 19 years, John proposed going to town officials and persuading them to reduce taxes and licenses, "given how little the show is; how we're just a bunch of kids" although of course he and his brothers were well acquainted with the ways of the circus and its audience. This strategy of choosing the most efficient routes and getting into profitable territories with a minimum of expense was to prove effective not only for the circus but for John in the long term as he pulled ahead financially and began to acquire his own fortune.

A SLOG TOWARD SUCCESS

During the 1885 season, the circus (because elephants be darned, that's exactly what it was) "played six days a week for twenty weeks without a break or single missed performance . . . a different stand every day for one hundred and twenty days," writes Plowden. Like the postal service, no Midwestern town was too big or too small, nor the weather too inclement. And during that and the following year, tents, acts, and other entertainments were added, and the circus began to break even, at times showing a profit. Although the brothers—including John, who, despite his budding entrepreneurship, continued his duties as the "Emperor of all Dutch dialect comedians, in his funny Dutchey maneuvers" and Alf T.

Portrait of John as a young blood. He surpassed his brothers in some ways but not in others.
THE JOHN AND MABLE RINGLING MUSEUM OF ART ARCHIVES, PAPERS OF JOHN RING-
LING, COLLECTION OF RINGLING FAMILY PHOTOGRAPHIC ALBUMS

and Charles, "who were billed as playing twelve different musical instruments." There were others as well, including Rich Dialo (real name: James Richardson), aka "The Human Volcano," who made quite an impression—in more ways than one—by "biting off bars of red-hot iron, eating boiling and blazing sealing wax," and finishing his performance by inviting an audience member to "melt lead and pour it into his mouth." Yum!

Another coup d'état of sorts, along with a basic menagerie of a bear, monkeys, lions, a trick Shetland pony, and others, was the "Hideous Hyena—Striata Gigantium The Mammoth, Marauding, Man-eating Monstrosity, the prowling, grave-robbing Demon of all Created Things, who while the World Sleeps, sneaks stealthily under cover of Darkness to the Cemetery and with Ghoulish Glee robs the Tomb. His Hideous Laughter paralyzes with Terror the Bravest Hearts. He leaves behind him a trail of blood; and the Wails of the Dying are Music to his Ear." Even if the hyena was having a less than amusing day, the hype alone undoubtedly struck fear into the hearts of the mostly rural, entertainment-starved population; reviews of the circus were mostly good, and audiences continued to flock there. And of course, the parade as they rolled into town added street cred and promotional value. Also of note was the fact that the forward-thinking Ringlings hired "the Dude," a Black comedian although he was often referred to in less than desirable terms.

1888 WAS A VERY GOOD (?) . . . WELL, IT WAS A YEAR

Given the Ringlings' continued momentum—by 1887, they were venturing as far as Nebraska, Kansas, and Missouri—it was only a matter of time before an elephant (actually two) came onto the scene. In 1888, John went to Frankfort, Illinois, to check out a sheriff's sale and came back with two pachyderms, Babylon and Fannie, whose cost was said to range from a thousand dollars for both to two thousand dollars each, depending on the source. By

1892, they owned six and by 1902, a mind-boggling herd of 40. Also,

> Two camels, Sampson and Queen, also joined the circus, as well as a "Zebu" [humped cow] and an emu. The new Big Top was 148 by 100 feet. There was also a menagerie top, three horse tops, and—unparalleled luxury—a dressing-room tent. Ringling Brothers had a real circus now, and they put the price of admission up to fifty cents (twenty-five cents for children). This was the standard charge for all full-grown circuses and remained the same for twenty or thirty years. (Ringling North, *The Circus Kings*, 68)

But that year, the brothers also encountered some major road-blocks. Excessive rains hampered the spring shows, damaging equipment and emptying the tents of audiences, "the worst experience in business since we started," wrote Otto in his request for a $1,000 bank loan. Otto continued:

> You cannot form any idea of the strain on us with everything at stake in the rain and mud all day and night for over a week. After Reedsburg [Wisconsin] it was almost unbearable, those clay hills were almost impassable. The wagons would sink down to the hubs and the poor horses could not budge them. We had to hire farmers . . . to help us with their horses and we had to put all our men to work with shovels to get the clay away from the wheels. Our repair bills . . . were enormous. Wagons continually pulled to pieces, springs broken, etc. (Ringling North, *The Circus Kings*, 69–70)

The murder of Dialo/Richardson/"The Human Volcano" on June 23 provided another unwelcome diversion. Apparently the result of a saloon brawl, which extended onto circus grounds, his killer, barkeep Thomas Baskett, was sentenced to 15 years in prison. Additionally, Al Ringling's wife, Louise, whom he'd married five years earlier, was kicked in the head by a horse. Lou, as she was known, had proven herself invaluable; she "made most of the costumes, cooked for all hands, and acted as adviser and house mother to the female performers, and was the star equestrienne" and "when necessity arose . . . even did some snake charming," notes Ringling North.

"The immense crowd thought she was killed as she was carried out of the ring to the dressing pavilion," writes Apps. Fortunately, she was only stunned and not injured, much to the relief of everyone concerned.

But that was also the year that Charles married Edith Conway, a preacher's daughter from Baraboo. Like Louise, Edith "traveled with the show and . . . worked hard at repairing costumes and sometimes took tickets at the door," continued Ringling North. John was not to meet his life partner, Mable Burton, until almost two decades later. Like Charles and Louise, they also became a power couple, especially in Sarasota in the early 20th century.

The Ringlings developed a code of ethics:

> [They] were well aware that some circuses and other traveling amusement enterprises had mottled reputations—infested with pickpockets who worked on a commission; ticket sellers and others who shortchanged patrons or even passed counterfeit money; "Monday men" who stole clothes off lines or burglarized homes while occupants [were] watching the parade or attended the performance.
>
> "Fixers" bribed officials to wink at petty crimes. They settled claims, when they must, in the quickest and easiest way possible, with glib promises. Often a complaining patron would be shuttled from one man to another until his patience wore out, or be told that "the man who handles that is not here, but he will be here tonight." (Plowden, *Those Amazing Ringlings*, 66–67)

The Victorian-era equivalent of an outsourced customer service center. . . . In addition to banning profanity, the brothers also drew up a set of rules of conduct for employees (mostly women)

Five bros, female pulchritude, and what today might be interpreted as a dodgy clown helped make the Ringling circus catnip to the late 1800s crowd.
LIBRARY OF CONGRESS

to be obeyed at all times and places. Along with "protecting" the females by providing an 11:00 p.m. curfew and dress code, no dating or even accidental meetings were tolerated, although of course the scanty costumes remained. Ushers and ticket sellers dressed in sharp-looking gold and blue uniforms and stood erect, with military bearing "Yes sir'ing" and "ma'am'ing" all comers.

The circus was shuttered on Sunday, earning the Ringlings the industry sobriquet "Sunday school boys," which worked in their favor, adding an evergreen sheen to their family-friendly image.

George Ade, a noted journalist, playwright, and author of that time period wrote, "They [the Ringlings] found the business in the hands of vagabonds and put it into the hands of gentlemen. . . . [They] became circus kings of the world by adopting and observing the simple rule that it is better to be straight than crooked." Of course, not all circuses employed skeezy practices—even the phrase "There's a sucker born every minute" has been incorrectly attributed to showman P. T. Barnum—an aura of disreputability hung around most circuses like a bad odor, which, through consistent practices and diligence, the Ringlings did much to dispel.

Burgeoned by profits and popularity, John began to look for innovative ways to supersize their footprint. For him and his brothers, it was beginning to look a lot like Christmas.

FROM WAGONS TO RAILROADS

In 1890, an ad ran in the *New York Clipper*, an entertainment trade magazine. "The Ringling Brothers Great United Circus and Menagerie" was selling all its wagon equipment to make way for a conversion to rail. All the successful circuses of the day traveled in this manner, including of course, P. T. Barnum, who had started the trend eight years earlier. Not only would this put the Ringlings in the "big boys club," but it would make circus life so much easier: "No more mud and dust. No more walking fifteen, twenty miles a day, usually at night and half asleep through the dark and gloom

. . . to the next town."They could reach larger audiences and travel farther, including into competitors' territories.

The brothers had also purchased a large home for their parents in Baraboo and were becoming an influence in that small community, leasing land and buildings to store equipment and animals and hiring staff to tend to business, off-season and on. Notes Ringling North, "This was the era when they introduced on their letterheads and advertising the famous picture of . . . the five partner-brothers all with seemingly identical profiles and those magnificent mustaches." Yet:

> they ranged in height from Charlie's neat five feet eight to Henry's elephantine six feet three. Their faces, unmasked, were equally disparate. Al's was thin and eager, at least in his youth. Gus had the visionary expression of a poet. Alf T. appeared to be determinedly businesslike, whereas Charles looked like the well-groomed sportsman of the Gay Nineties. Otto's face wore a banker's solid look. John, the only one with curly hair, had the round-faced, round-eyed humorous expression which had set the farmers laughing in the prairie village hall, whereas Henry, though also round-faced, was beetle-browed and slightly sinister. (Ringling North, *The Circus Kings*, 74)

They also expanded in other ways. Physically, because most of them became overweight due to all the rich meals they could now afford—not to mention those big cigars, which did little for their health—but also in terms of different hobbies and tastes. "When money gave them freedom of choice each went his separate way in private life, though they remained indissolubly bound together in the partnership," added Ringling North. Of course, like most families, especially those in business, there were the inevitable arguments and heated disagreements, but by all accounts, they got along well during those early years.

Although they presented a united front, the brothers were very different, as this circa 1895 family portrait aptly illustrates.
THE JOHN AND MABLE RINGLING MUSEUM OF ART ARCHIVES, PAPERS OF JOHN N. RINGLING, COLLECTION OF RINGLING FAMILY PHOTOGRAPHIC ALBUMS

During this period, John began to come into his own. Aided by Otto, he engineered the purchase of surplus railroad equipment from a competitor, the Adam Forepaugh Circus, a total of 18 cars, 2 advance and 16 for the circus itself. Among the latter were "one performer's sleeper, one workingman's sleeper, one elephant car, five stock cars [for animals] and eight flatcars [for equipment]."

This was the first step in what would become an eventual takeover of the circus world. While other circuses struggled, folding and consolidating, the Ringlings continued to gain steam, expanding their reach to the entire United States and eventually, Europe; booking exotic acts from overseas; acquiring unusual and at the time barely heard of animals—for example, a "Blood Sweating" hippopotamus—and creating larger and ever more elaborate extravaganzas. (For the record, hippos don't actually sweat blood but instead, secrete a reddish oily fluid, which serves as a water repellent, skin moisturizer, and antibiotic. Of course, early explorers didn't know that, and the Ringlings, true to form, stuck with what was commonly believed to be the truth.)

The move to rails demarcated a big leap for John as well.

This was a very intricate job, essential to the success of a season. . . . [I]t meant planning the exact time of each section every day in co-operation with dozens of railroads and hundreds of branch lines. Uncle John's prodigious memory became practically a railroad guide to the United States. For example, if you wondered in his presence how best you could get from Altoona, Pennsylvania, to North Yakima, Washington, he would instantly come up with train times, junction points, and connections. One of his favorite tricks was to let you name a railroad and time-table, and then stick a nail file into the Consolidated Railway Guide, as thick as the New York telephone book, and come within a page or two. (Ringling North, *The Circus Kings*, 76)

In 1906, Ringling acquired what was by then called the Forepaugh-Sells Circus and a year later, the Barnum & Bailey Circus. Initially, the latter was kept separate from Ringling, touring different parts of the country and with about the same number of employees, animals, and acts, but in 1919, eight years before John Ringling moved their headquarters to Sarasota, they merged and became known as the "Ringling Bros. and Barnum & Bailey Combined Shows" and were billed as "The Greatest Show on Earth," with the Ringling name first, of course.

Managing and organizing where the circus was supposed to come and go allowed John to expand his considerable management skills and circle of contacts, eventually leading to investments in real estate and the U.S. economy that cemented his fortunes, at least until the 1929 stock market crash. This also helped set the stage for one-of-a-kind acquisitions that would become the huge complex known as the John and Mable Ringling Museum of Art, putting Sarasota on the cultural map.

Chapter 6

Marriage and Love
MABLE AND SARASOTA

In 1905, when John Ringling married Mable Burton, the circus was at its apex of independent success, "arguably the most successful circus ever," notes Jerry Apps in *Ringlingville, USA*. It continued to expand—three nonstop rings of "elephant and horse acts, acrobats, aerialists, jugglers, and horse races of several stripes: monkeys riding Shetland ponies, a ladies' jockey race, a four-horse Roman chariot race," and more drawn from exotic corners of the Earth. "Tableau wagons" with ornate, guilded carvings from

Gilded circus wagons such as these have been beautifully restored and now live in the Circus Museum at the Ringling.
SANDRA GURVIS

Russia and Germany; flatbed wagons representing Egypt, France, and Persia; and cages with their impressive displays of lions, tigers, and hippos—oh my!—kept audiences coming back for more.

THE BROS LEVEL UP

The dawning years of the 20th century saw the premiere of the "Ringling Brothers World's Greatest Shows and the Libretto of the Sublime Spectacle Jerusalem and the Crusades"—which while along with competing with Barnum & Bailey, which they purchased in 1907 and others, threw in a troupe of 95 ballerinas in the hopes of giving vaudeville a run for its money. Along with crowds, reviewers went wild, calling it "the most complete and startling arenic [*sic*] performance in the world . . . on a scale of grandeur and magnificence never before attempted," although Apps pointed out that "one wonders how many of these were written by Alf T. Ringling or one of his press agents and presented to the paper in a tidy package," which can sometimes wander into the territory of what is now known as "fake news."

By now, all the brothers had married and had families, except John and Otto, who remained stubbornly single, but for vastly different reasons. In 1883, Gus joined Al, Charles, and Henry in holy matrimony by marrying Quebec-born Anna Herley, and in 1890, Alf T. wed Della Andrews of Baraboo.

While Otto stayed "a skinflinty bachelor," according to Gene Plowden in *Those Amazing Ringlings and Their Circus*, and lived at Al's house in Baraboo when he wasn't on the road so as to save on rent or a mortgage, John was his diametrical opposite, at least in terms of lifestyle. Like the rest of his brothers and their families, John traveled around the country in a luxurious private railroad car—a practical necessity of circus life—but he also used his travels for other means.

His eyes were always searching for opportunity. He loved money more than anything except pictures, and he never

By the time John met Mable, he was a major success in his own right.
THE JOHN AND MABLE RINGLING MUSEUM OF ART ARCHIVES, PAPERS OF JOHN
RINGLING, COLLECTION OF RINGLING FAMILY PHOTOGRAPHIC ALBUMS

missed a chance of making some. He might see a theater in some small city that was doing badly and could be
turned into a profitable movie house; or a streetcar line
that needed a little capital; or even a steam laundry whose

owner wanted to retire. It did not matter to Uncle John what the line was as long as there was money in it. As a result, he owned businesses all over the United States. (Ringling North, *The Circus Kings*, 105–106)

John also built railroads and bought up oil leases and by the time he met Mable, was well on his way to the financial stratosphere today inhabited by Jeff Bezos and Bill Gates. Unlike his brothers, who continued to be deeply involved with the circus, "John began to move into more conventional business arenas," noted David Weeks in *Ringling: The Florida Years*. As the years went on, "he was often miles away, dealing with rail executives, Interstate Commerce Commission officials, and others to whom the circus was an alien world." He continued to build his wealth through these and other investments, including purchasing land in and around Sarasota and elsewhere, holding positions in an estimated total of 35 companies.

His roving eye extended to women as well. By all accounts, John was a player, squiring around showgirls and other sorts of fancy ladies, although, according to Ringling North, he never ate where he hunted because it "gave him too great an advantage and that it was unsporting, like shooting a sitting bird." Okaay . . . Ringling North also pointed out that even after John's marriage to Mable, although he treated her with devotion and respect, when he was out of her sightline on his many trips,

He was apt to relapse into his bachelor ways. With far more wisdom than most women, Aunt Mable realized that her husband was too old and gay a dog to learn new tricks of behavior. She treated his infidelities as though they had never happened. So, of course, they did not exist for her. In this she was far more intelligent than Aunt Edith, who soured her happiness with constant worry about what Uncle Charlie might be up to. (Ringling North, *The Circus Kings*, 124)

A MEETUP MYSTERY

How John met Mable is the object of much speculation, as is Mable herself. Born Armilda Burton on March 4, 1875, in the farming community of Moons, Ohio, near what is now Washington Courthouse, she had four sisters and one brother, with whom she remained close throughout her lifetime. Perhaps because she and John never had children of their own and also because her marriage to him allowed her to afford it, she took stewardship of her family: raising three of her sisters' children, providing them with the best education possible and offering financial and other assistance to the rest. Attractive and charming,

> she had a lovely, piquant little face with delicate features and large brown eyes that always seemed to have laughter close behind them, just as her lips always seemed to be on the point of smiling. Her dark hair was piled in a Gibson-girl pompadour. She had the figure known as willowy and was able to wear the long elaborate gowns of the Edwardian era with beauty and distinction. (Ringling North, *The Circus Kings*, 123)

Yet Mable was also intensely private, cultivating an air of almost mystery, which seemed to surround her the moment she met John when she was in her late 20s, nearly a spinster by that era's standards, and he was 37. While rumors that she had been a performer in the Ringling circus were largely debunked, her sister, Amanda Wortman, asserted that John first encountered Mable in 1903 when she was cashiering in a restaurant during the Chicago World's Fair, which might have involved time travel since that event had happened a decade earlier. Mable's sister-in-law (married to her brother, Earl) told the *Sarasota Herald-Tribune* that she was "positive" the couple had met in Atlantic City. "She had previously worked in a shoe factory and was working in a small jewelry stand. . . . John courted her on the boardwalk and lavished money on her."

By all accounts, Mable Ringling was quite a looker.
PHOTO COURTESY OF THE SARASOTA COUNTY HISTORY CENTER

The latter part was definitely true and marked the beginning of a long, prosperous, and on this, accounts mostly agree, amenable and smooth-running marriage. Intelligent, poised, "and blessed with a warm personality that nicely balanced her husband's habitual reserve," according to Weeks, the two shared many mutual passions and interests, including art, travel, and culture, especially all things Italian, which would prove to be a huge boon for Sarasota.

The affinity for mutual grandiloquence exhibited itself when John kitted out their railroad car, "one of the finest . . . [with] plush red velvet and brass trimmings," noted Plowden, ornately signifying it with the name "JomaR," a combination of "John" and "Mable" with "R" for "Ringling," proving once again that history repeats and the invention of "Brangelina" was not a product of the 21st century.

According to the *Sarasota Herald-Tribune*, in its heyday, JomaR "also carried around the likes of President Harding and General Pershing, but the train was abandoned in the mid-1900s and eventually became the property of a law firm in Sarasota."

Today, JomaR—or at least a part of it—lives on in Bob's Train, a Sarasota restaurant/museum. SANDRA GURVIS

When not on the road, the John Ringlings also resided in a toney hotel apartment in downtown Chicago, moving even further up the social ladder to the Big Apple in 1910, purchasing an even more elaborate place on Fifth Avenue.

It was as if they were preparing for their own grand finale that would forever change many lives and the city of Sarasota. "At the time of their marriage, John was gaining affluence, but he derived most of his income from the circus rather than the multiple interests that later helped to make him rich," observed Weeks. "For several years Mable took advantage of the quiet interval between seasons to be tutored" almost as if she was preparing herself for what was to come. Along with the art museum, the gardens, and many other places in and around the area, their most notable achievement would be Ca' d'Zan, their world-famous Mediterranean revival residence, which not surprisingly translates into "House of John."

When "JomaR" Met Sarasota

In the early 1900s, the brothers "turned to Florida as an alternative to the wintry blasts of Chicago and Wisconsin," noted Weeks, continuing:

> The months when the circuses were in winter quarters allowed the owners to enjoy the dual luxury of leisure time and freedom from the demands of almost daily travel. However, the unconventional life of the circus tended to separate even the proprietors from society in general. Florida offered a welcome change from the rapacious demands of circus life on the road.
>
> Florida's potential as a market for the largest circus shows in the country was coupled with the improved national economy, which had recovered from the losses suffered in the panic of 1907. Several new stands [venues], such as Tampa, were added to the itinerary. (Weeks, *Ringling: The Florida Years*, 65)

By 1910, they were juggling three circuses: Ringling Brothers, Barnum & Bailey—which had 84 railcars each—and the smaller Forepaugh-Sells circus with 47 cars. While this period brought prosperity, it also initiated competition—from the burgeoning "moving picture" industry, although with his usual foresight and cool calculation, John had invested in movie houses; to the Victrola record player with its potential to access an array of music and in-home entertainment; to the "horseless carriages," which increasingly crowded the roads thanks to Henry Ford's mass production. Along with allowing for even greater mobility, the latter "[made] it difficult to mount a circus parade," noted Apps.

The innovations opened up even more options for stage shows and vaudeville "as communities built opera houses and traveling . . . troupes traipsed across the country entertaining huge numbers of rural and small town people," which for decades had made up the Ringlings' base audience. And while "the circus rolled on, much as it had since pre-Civil War days" with animals, parades, aerialists, and ringmasters, and "crowds continued to come . . . the Ringling Brothers, now the undisputed kings of the circus world, had to be highly concerned about the changes . . . going on around them," continued Apps.

It was into this environment that John and Mable dipped their toes into Sarasota. "For one or two seasons, John and Mable tested the life-style of winter residents at Tarpon Springs, then a sport fishing resort north of Tampa," observed Weeks. "The rich sportsmen wintering there formed a small, closed community. This exclusive company was cool to "new money" and disinclined to accept circus people," although by that time, John Ringling hardly fell into that category. Noted journalist Martha Dreiblatt wrote,

> John Ringling in no way resembles the traditional showman. He has none of the gay garrulity, the extravagances and eccentricities of a man like, say, P. T. Barnum. There is a reticence, almost a sardonic reticence about him, a

great sense of physical power and energy, and with all that charm which all men must have whose success depends on domineering people and making them like it. (*Brooklyn Daily Eagle*, July 14, 1929, 5)

Nor was John one to be shunted aside or to change his ways to accommodate people who believed themselves to be his betters. Instead, thanks to the influence of his friends, railroad executive Ralph Caples and circus manager Charles Thompson, whose long game was to get John and Charles Ringling to move to their hood anyway, John was invited to check out their Sarasota homes near Indian Beach, a leisurely day cruise on John and Mable's yacht, Louise II.

Caples himself had discovered Sarasota in 1899 "by horse and buggy, on a delayed honeymoon trip through Florida," according to Sarasota History Alive! He and his wife, Ellen, fell in love with the place and wintered there, moving permanently to Shell Beach in 1909.

His principal role in Sarasota was that of a civic leader, an unpaid publicist for the city, and a promoter of local participation in ventures initiated by developers. . . . [H]e liked to display a visible presence in local charity efforts during the Depression, when hardship was common in the homes of many local families. Ellen Caples, like her husband, was a central figure in the society that brought together the local elites and the wealthy new families from the North. (Weeks, *Ringling: The Florida Years*, 65)

Through various machinations, and even though his own company, the Florida West Coast Railroad, failed in its attempt, Caples, who had been successful in other ventures, "managed to get the railroad to come to Sarasota years earlier than it would have," noted Sarasota History Alive!

Since Thompson also had a background in circus management, he "assured John and Mable that they would not find there the same unfriendly bias and social barriers encountered in Tarpon Springs," stated Weeks.

Once John decided on the area, however, he, his family, and his friends traded houses and land as easily as people used to swap baseball cards.

> On November 3, 1911, Caples bought the Thompson home and some additional land. Caples sold the Thompson estate less than three months later to John Ringling. After selling his home Thompson built a second home next to it. He sold other sections of his land to Charles Ringling. . . . Ultimately, he sold the site of his second home to Charles Ringling so that he could build a home for his daughter, Hester Ringling Sanford. (Weeks, *Ringling: The Florida Years*, 67)

John originally purchased 20 acres from Charles Thompson, but that was just the beginning of the Ringling tsunami of land acquisition.

John and Mable likely also felt the need to settle down, to have something more permanent and personal than a fancy apartment or railroad car. In their case, of course, it would be in addition to these things. Eventually, they would come to see Sarasota as the blank slate onto which they could carve an outrageously extravagant and unique lifestyle.

JOHN AND MABLE AND CHARLES AND EDITH

Not only did Charles and Edith soon purchase a Sarasota house for themselves almost adjacent to John and Mable's, but the surviving brothers pretty much followed suit—Al and wife, Louise, rented a winter home in Sarasota, and Alf T. and his second wife, Elizabeth (he and Della divorced in 1914), bought an estate from

The Last Curtain Call for the First Ringling Circus Generation

Like all siblings, the Ringling brothers fought, and like many, it was usually behind closed doors. They presented a united front to the world, especially important in a business where rivals circled like sharks and any hint of divisiveness was as attractive as the scent of blood. In late 1906, the still intact family unit gathered together in Baraboo for a festive last supper. In fragile health herself, "Mama Rüngling sat at the table, beaming her happiness," states Plowden. "'Here are my boys,' she said. 'I never was happier in my life.'" She died a few weeks later.

Slowly, the tight skein that made up the Ringling fabric began to unravel. Although only five—Al, Alf T., Otto, John, and Charles—were full partners, Gus worked in advertising and Henry served as an advance man during the early years, although according to Ringling North, he struggled with alcoholism and depression. Gus, the second oldest, was the first to pass away, in 1907, of Bright's disease at age 53. Now referred to as nephritis, back then it was a blanket term for kidney inflammation caused by infections, toxins, or autoimmune disorders.

Bright's was to fell two other Ringling brothers: Otto, also 53, in 1911, and Al, five years later when he was 66. Otto's death had a big impact. Not only was the famous trademark advertisement of the five mustachioed brothers pulled from the advertising lineup, but the Forepaugh-Sells circus, which Gus had also managed, was closed; Otto and Al left their shares to the remaining brothers—Alf T., John, Charles, and Henry, who had only worked for the circus but upon Otto's passing, was made a full partner.

Several of the Ringlings passed from heart disease and/or stroke: Henry, at age 49 in 1918; Alf T., at 56 in 1919; and Ida Ringling North, at 76 in 1950. The remaining two brothers, who were the longest lived males, were Charles, who died in 1926 of pneumonia at age 63, and John, also of pneumonia almost exactly 10 years later to the day at 70. (Talk about odd coincidences!) But it was Alf T.'s death that truly narrowed the field and sowed the seeds for future discontent. He left his one-third ownership of the conglomerate—Charles and John also owned a third—to his son, Richard.

a former Confederate general. The only holdout was Henry, who although he and Ida wintered in Eustis about 150 miles away, they visited Sarasota frequently enough that according to Weeks, "[they] left their launch Salomé at the John Ringling dock for Mable's pleasure."

Even their sister, Ida Ringling North, got into the act, wintering in Sarasota, eventually moving into the "Winter White House" in Bird Key, shortly after John's death. Built in 1910 by Thomas Worcester of Cincinnati as a retirement home for him and his wife, Davie, the luxurious estate was also known as the Worchester mansion and New Edzell Castle. John purchased it in the early 1920s, with ambitions of hosting then-president Warren G. Harding.

When it came to Sarasota, however, it was essentially the John and Mable and Charles and Edith show.

> Their nearly adjoining Florida homes suggest not only that they were compatible companions, but also that they were accustomed to and preferred a close family circle as the center of their domestic and social life. Charles built a frame house large enough for his family of four and a few occasional visitors. From the outset, the difference in the personalities of the two brothers was visible in the plans for their new homes. John Ringling began at once to improve the landscaping; he removed utility buildings from view and generally made certain that "Palms Elysian," as the house was known, would become a showplace. In contrast, Charles planted a small grove of citrus trees, and added a token harness shop (as a reminder of his apprentice days) and a barn for his cows. (Weeks, *Ringling: The Florida Years*, 68)

But tension was brewing underneath the surface, especially when it came to life in Paradise:

There had never been anything but love and loyalty between the Ringling brothers until Alf T. died. But when Charles and John were left to divide their world between them, a ground mist of jealousy rose to cloud their relationship. This did not affect their management of the circus. There, as always, they acted in concert. But in their outside business ventures and their social life, the rivalry between them became more acute, even bitter. John Ringling went his own freewheeling way, and his wife Mable was very easygoing and still one of the most beautiful women in America; but Edith, though handsome, was gray-haired and matronly. She kept prodding Charles to outdo his rambunctious younger brother. (Ringling North, *The Circus Kings*, 145)

According to John's grandniece, Pat Ringling Buck, the wives differed in other ways as well. "Despite her elegant appearance, Mable Ringling was not a hot house flower," she recounted in her memoir *The Ringling Legacy*. "She liked to fish and was a good shot." The latter extended to the snakes and other critters that had the audacity to show themselves while the home and museum were being built. She also had "a great talent and love for gardening," discussed further in chapter 8.

Although Mable had little to do with her husband's actual business dealings, her reach extended far beyond their (very huge) backyard. Although by all accounts, generally press and camera-shy and somewhat reserved when out in public, she was civic-minded and made major design contributions to the museum, Ca' d'Zan, and various properties in and around the region.

In contrast, although family oriented, especially when their children, Robert and Hester were growing up, Edith Ringling was highly involved with the circus. The former teacher and preacher's daughter, "traveled with the show nearly every year until 1950, except for a period after Charles' death in 1926," states Sarasota

History Alive! And this was during a time when women, particularly married ones, were rarely seen in the workforce.

Little did John, Charles, and their families know that what was about to unfold would represent a much wilder ride.

Baraboo Booster: Al, Ringlingville, and "America's Prettiest Playhouse"

Of all the brothers and their wives, the also-childless Al and Louise "were so immersed in the circus that they were never content to be far from its sights and sounds," noted Weeks. "They hastened to Baraboo early each spring before going on the road with one of the shows." Baraboo appreciated their native son as well. The former Al Ringling Mansion is a favorite tourist attraction, and there's even an Al Ringling Brewing Co., which offers libations and food.

In 1915, Al also built what locals like to refer to as "America's Prettiest Playhouse." With a cost of $100,000—the equivalent of about $4 million today—the Al Ringling Theatre originally seated 874 and was modeled after the opera house at Versailles, not surprising considering the family penchant for all things rococo. Remodeled in 2016, it is still in use and on the National Register of Historic Places.

Baraboo is also the site of "Ringlingville," the original winter headquarters, where the brothers stored animals and equipment. Ten of the original 25 structures remain standing today, according to Sauk County records, the largest conglomeration of its kind in the country and part of the Circus World Museum. In 1918, Ringling winter quarters was moved to the old P. T. Barnum property in Bridgeport, Connecticut, and then nine years later, to Sarasota.

RING THREE
The Ringling Effect

Chapter 7

Those Amazing Ringlings and Their Fabulous (Dueling) Houses, Yachts, and Business Interests

The Roaring '20s set the stage for a spectacular extravaganza of Ringling land purchases, property development, and wildly luxurious houses and yachts, with much accompanying hoopla. "Sarasotans, twenty-four of them, were 'made' into overnight movie performers yesterday afternoon when a Fox News cameraman . . . took scenes aboard John Ringling's palatial yacht the 'Zalophus,'" proclaimed the March 9, 1927, *Sarasota Herald-Tribune*. The story went on to explain that the newsreel would be shown in "several thousand" movie houses and "undoubtedly be seen by millions of theatre-goers" throughout the nation. Other stops included the now-defunct El Vernona Hotel, the recently completed John Ringling Causeway, and Lido Beach—all John's and to a lesser extent, Charles's kingdom, although unfortunately Charles had passed away the year before. Although the El Vernona was owned by Owen Burns when the newsreel was filmed, John purchased it when it went bankrupt after the stock market crash of 1929.

While John cultivated the patronage of the powerful, wealthy, and elite, he was also savvy enough to know that in addition to the actual little people who populated his circus—some of whom followed the winter circus when it moved to Sarasota in 1927—other "little people" were needed to make his slice of paradise a viable operation.

A boat ride was often part of the deal when prospects went to check out the Sarasota area.

In 1923 more than three and a half million spectators, three-fourths of them adults, attended the circus. That amounted to one in thirty among the country's entire population. Countless others saw the Ringling Bros.

posters. The new campaign promoted Sarasota's seaside charms and sports attractions: "Spend a Summer this Winter in Sarasota." On placards in hotels, terminals, and store windows—in any public place that would permit them—the Ringling message was broadcast. For the first time, much of the nation became aware of Sarasota and the then-developing Florida dream. (Weeks, *Ringling: The Florida Years*, 121)

THE RINGLING LAND GRAB

In the1920s, John Ringling and to a lesser extent Charles and their cohort of wealthy white men made it their mission to purchase as much land as cheaply as possible. Bertha Palmer, the only female influencer of that era, had passed away in 1918, so it's doubtful she ever met any of the Ringlings.

But unlike John's usual over-the-(big)top style, the takeover was gradual. "[John] started slowly, more as a speculation than as part of a concerted plan," states Weeks. His first purchase, in 1916, was of the bankrupt Sarasota Yacht and Automobile Club, a good choice because he needed a place to park his tub. A few months later, according to Sarasota History Alive!, he also acquired what's now known as Golden Gate Point, located across from Cedar Key.

His main contact was local magnate and builder Owen Burns, whom John met through his early real estate dealings. This marked the beginning of a long and fruitful relationship, although "because of [John's] sporadic presence in Sarasota, few could have known much of his business personality, of his unusual work habits, or of the strange hours he kept when he worked at night and slept all day," continued Weeks. "Burns must indeed have been a man of infinite patience, for he would need it." The partnership grew as John spent more time in Sarasota, although "they left few records of their joint projects and still fewer of their disagreements."

No one was immune from John's idiosyncrasies, including Charles. "One way in which Charles indicated his disapproval of his brother's offbeat hours was always to make business appointments with him at nine o'clock in the morning, knowing full well that he [John] habitually breakfasted at three in the afternoon," noted Henry Ringling North in *The Circus Kings*. "John was invariably late for ordinary business conferences; in fact, his tardiness at one vital meeting helped to bring about his financial downfall."

Although "Charles [was] a gentleman who always avoided giving offense," observed Weeks, he "permitted himself only one burst of indirect candor to describe his brother" writing "'ME, ME, ME,' next to John's name on an early circus roster." Some things never change.

John also enlisted Mable as a partner in his real estate holdings, although "[that] inclusion . . . was altogether contrary to Ringling's beliefs about the role of women," added Weeks. "He needed a third member of his firm, yet he did not have enough confidence in any other Sarasota businessman to share even a limited knowledge of his financial affairs." As a result, Mable's primary role was in designing and decorating various interiors and exteriors, including John's business office and the eventual conversion of the yacht club into apartments for winter visitors.

In early 1923, John and Charles became directors at the Bank of Sarasota, of which John was a principal. A few months earlier they had each purchased some 33,000 acres (66,000 total) in southeastern Sarasota County. John also bought approximately 1,000 acres closer to the city in what is now known as the Tamiami Trail. Although sources such as Weeks estimate that they paid close to $1 an acre—probably realistic since land was at bargain basement prices thanks to the hurricane of 1921—others claimed that some serious horse trading was going on:

> One night during a poker game in Montgomery, Alabama, John bought a block of land in what was to become the southern part of Sarasota County. . . . Before going to bed, he telephoned Charles and insisted that they go in

together on the deal and split the cost. Charles sleepily argued that he wasn't even at the poker game and knew nothing of the land but John persisted and had his way. A short time later John was in Sarasota and went to see his good friend, Arthur B. Edwards, a native and the town's first mayor. "I've got 66,000 acres of land down there around the Myakka River," John said. "Bought it off of a senator up in Alabama."

"That's fine, Mr. Ringling," Edwards replied. "I hope you didn't pay too much for it."

"Oh, I didn't pay much. How much you think it's worth, A. B.?"

"I'd say a dollar seventy-five, maybe two dollars an acre. If you paid more than that you got stuck. Mind telling me what you had to give for it, Mr. Ringling?"

"Two and a quarter."

"You did? Why, I had that land listed for a long time. I could have got it for you for a dollar seventy-five."

"You could?" John whined. "By God, A. B.; I've been clipped sure as hell. I thought I was getting a bargain, but he hooked me good and proper." (Plowden, *Those Amazing Ringlings and Their Circus*, 140–41)

While this may be the stuff of legend, it fueled the hype over John Ringling's wealth and contributed to the rivalry between him and Charles. "The burden of running the unwieldy circus organization had fallen more heavily on Charles as John spent more time on his other burgeoning interests," noted Weeks. "Charles's resentment grew as his brother did less of the work but still maintained his domineering attitudes." Few if any outsiders were aware of this, "although some in Sarasota and in the circus sensed the tensions below an amicable surface."

And it wasn't only the Ringling performers who knew how to juggle:

Few would know that [John] was often in need of cash, which was frequently borrowed or contrived from manipulating movable assets. An important part of Ringling's real estate strategy . . . was to invest in grandiose landscaping projects. From a nursery on Longboat Key, he moved hundreds of palms and exotic plants to his own estate and to his other property on the keys. His intent was to give his estate and the keys a thoroughly tropical appearance as an inducement to northern buyers. Prospective buyers were not asked to visualize a "someday" Florida community; they were to see carefully planned landscaping already in place. (Weeks, *Ringling: The Florida Years*, 114)

This ability to understand audience need was a hallmark of all the Ringling undertakings, enhancing their appeal and greatly contributing to their eventual success.

Ever the impresario, John understood the psychology of—to mix a couple of cliches—showing the goods before sealing the deal.
THE JOHN AND MABLE RINGLING MUSEUM OF ART ARCHIVES, PAPERS OF JOHN RINGLING, COLLECTION OF RINGLING FAMILY PHOTOGRAPHIC ALBUMS

Essentially John's strategy was simple: to purchase as much as possible of Longboat, St. Armands, Bird, Lido, and other adjoining land and keys. What was initially known as (but of course) Ringling Isles was to include "a causeway from the mainland, a grand boulevard to run the length of Longboat Key, a great hotel, a bathing pavilion, smart shops on St. Armand's Key," according to various newspaper accounts. The execution, of course, was far more complicated and involved massive amounts of wheeling and dealing.

A RIVALRY OF NONEPIC PROPORTIONS?

Their approach to various projects underscored the difference between the two brothers. Observed historian Jeff LaHurd, "'Mr. Charlie,' as the elder of the two was affectionately known, was a gentler soul. Kind and empathetic, he was not given to the stern lectures and domineering mannerisms of his brother. He was sought out for advice and counsel and was known for his charitable endeavors." Although LaHurd called him a "steadying influence," Charles also was not immune to the "he who dies with the most toys wins" mentality that would grip the country several decades later.

According to Ringling North, the tension between the two brothers reached its peak when they built their palatial homes "side by side facing the bay in Sarasota."

Uncle Charles began his in 1924, immediately after hearing of Uncle John's grandiose plans for a Venetian palazzo. Charles Ringling's home was, and still is, an uncommonly beautiful house. Following the classically simple lines of eighteenth-century English architecture, it was built of Georgia marble tinged by the palest shade of pink. The spacious, beautifully proportioned rooms were filled with appropriate graceful furniture built by Sheraton and Hepplewhite in England nearly two hundred years ago. Because

Charles and Edith's stunning home also faces the bay and is now part of the "liberal" arts New College of Florida.
SANDRA GURVIS

Charles Ringling loved music so much, he installed a magnificent organ, and the music room, with its carefully planned acoustics, was often filled by the voices of the great singers of the time, most of whom were his son Robert's friends. [Robert Ringling was a well-known opera singer.] Such a beautiful house . . . should have been enough to satisfy any man. (Ringling North, *The Circus Kings*, 146)

This brotherly one-upmanship also extended to their yachts: "If Uncle John got a yacht, the *Zalophus*, Uncle Charles had to have an even bigger one, the Symphonia," continued Ringling North, although by some accounts the *Zalophus* was the slightly larger and certainly more ostentatious. Along with telephone service, it boasted large bedrooms and oversized furniture with brass fittings and mahogany-paneled interiors suitable for ferrying the monied set. Prior to the 1926 completion of the causeway, one could only reach Ringling Isles by water.

The "tensions," such as they were, turned out to be moot, as Charles passed away unexpectedly a few months after his mansion was completed in 1926. Fortunately for his widow, Edith, who resided in the home until her 1953 death, daughter Hester and son Robert lived nearby, providing emotional support. Five years later, Charles's mansion along with 30 acres was sold to Sarasota Kennel Club owner Jerry Collins for the low, low price of $100,000; after renovation and restoration, Collins sold it in 1962 for a cool $4 million to the just-formed New College of Florida, where it now goes by the unassuming moniker of College Hall. However, unlike Ca' d'Zan, which charges admission and is strictly regulated, visitors can walk in during the college business hours and revel in at least some past Ringling glory.

Still, Charles's investments reflected his demurer, locally based approach and included, according to LaHurd, "what had previously been scrub-filled wasteland. The *Herald* credited Charles and his son-in-law, Louis Lancaster, for transforming a 'rubbish heap and sandy wastes into a Civic Center in two years.'" Additionally, Charles purchased the former golf course built by John Hamilton Gillespie and developed what was known as the Court House Subdivision, donating the land for the courthouse and building the 10-story, 125-room Sarasota Terrace Hotel, at the time, the city's tallest building. Continues LaHurd, "Across the street from the Terrace and constructed around the same time was the Charles Ringling Building, which, like the hotel, still stands . . . [what] the *Herald* described . . . as 'a small link in the mighty chain in the accomplishments of the Charles Ringling organization.'" Other buildings in Terrace Square included the University Club, the Triangle Drug Store, and the Clarence Saunders Grocery.

Along with being president of the Sarasota Chamber of Commerce, Charles also established the Ringling Trust and Savings, which during the Great Depression, did the right thing when Edith, using her own money, paid the depositors back in full, rather than the usual pennies on the dollar.

NO ELEPHANTS FOR THIS WATER

In the mid-1920s, the Florida land boom was in full swing, an almost-eerie echo of post-pandemic America—and Florida—nearly 100 years later. "The oil wells were pouring out their wealth; the railroads were running to the limit of capacity; theaters, turned into movie houses, were packing them in," states Ringling North. It was during this period that John Ringling undertook his three most ambitious projects: the building of Ca' d'Zan and the museum and the development of Ringling Isles. Of the latter, St. Armands, the causeway, and a much-anticipated Ritz Carlton formed the basis of unprecedented growth.

St. Armands Circle

In 1885, Frenchman Charles St. Amand purchased 130-plus acres of an uninhabited, oval-shaped island for $13—today the average price of a glass of wine in one of the Circle's many upscale restaurants. He hardly lived a luxurious lifestyle, "fishing in the waters of the Gulf and Bay . . . rais[ing] produce which he brought by boat to the market at City Pier in Sarasota," according to the St. Armands Circle Association. His name was misspelled as "St. Armand" on various deeds and never corrected.

Enter John Ringling, who bought the land in the early 1920s. His ambitions included resorts, a casino, residential lots, and a shopping center laid out in a circle with exits leading to Lido and Longboat keys, today a logistical traffic nightmare avoided by most locals who use the side streets. Ornamented with Italian statuary purchased from his many trips to Rome, Naples, and Venice, he named the main drag Harding Circle after his supposed buddy, President Warren G. Harding, with whom he allegedly broached the idea of establishing a winter White House on Bird Key. He also named streets after Harding and other presidents.

States historian Jeff LaHurd: "According to Ringling, the president loved the idea [of a Winter White House] and 'displayed all the enthusiasm of a big boy over his contemplated vacation in Sarasota.' Ringling noted that the president's desk was covered with pictures of the Ringling yacht *Zalophus*, which would be at his disposal during 'his sojourn on it as a haven of rest.'" It never came about, as Harding passed away unexpectedly in August 1923, amid what was popularly called the Teapot Dome scandal, which although it did not involve Harding directly, caused him a great deal of stress because his Secretary of the Interior was caught taking kickbacks for secretly leasing federal oil reserves to oil tycoons. (Things never really do change.) And whether Ringling and Harding actually met is uncertain, although they did have a mutual friend in circus executive Ralph Caples.

One circus meets another: John Ringling viewing the "Greatest Show on Earth" with President Calvin and First Lady Grace Coolidge in Washington, D.C.

"As no bridge to the key had yet been built, Ringling engaged an old paddle-wheel steamboat, the 'Success' to serve as a workboat," continued the St. Armands Circle Association. "His crews labored at dredging canals, building seawalls, and installing sidewalks and streets lined with rose-colored curbs," not unlike the figurative glasses John Ringling wore when touting his ambitions.

Ringling Causeway

In January 1924, plans were announced for what would eventually become the first of three versions of the Ringling Causeway, which connected St. Armands and the keys to the mainland.

Privately funded by John Ringling and others, the original two-mile drawbridge "of high span and great beauty and original design" was to be "one of the most distinctive of its kind in the United States," enthused the *Sarasota Times*.

Two years later, on January 1, 1926, John Ringling was the first to cross the bridge in his green Rolls-Royce limo. "Work continued until an hour before his crossing, when the last nail was driven into the planks of the draw span," noted Weeks. And while some sources claimed that circus elephants were used to haul the timbers that supported the concrete piles, that job was accomplished by a far less glamorous dredge—also named after John Ringling—owned by Owen Burns's construction company. Elephants were a high-maintenance, expensive commodity: even John Ringling himself refused to lend a single pachyderm to support his beloved Republican Party during its Diamond Jubilee, citing safety concerns. And elephants only came to Sarasota when circus winter quarters moved to town in 1927, the same year Ringling donated "his" bridge to the city.

On February 7, 1926, "the public got their chance to motor across Sarasota Bay," noted LaHurd. "For the grand opening, the Czecho-Slovakian band, hired by Ringling to add color and excitement to the festivities, gave rousing concerts in an especially constructed band shell on St. Armand's Circle."

The always savvy John also provided bus transportation to the island. "Before the day was over, thousands of locals and snowbirds had poured onto the key to be impressed by what the paper called a 'tropical utopia,'" LaHurd went on. "Ringling reportedly sold $1 million worth of property."

While at the time considered a genius feat of engineering, the bridge only lasted a few decades:

By the early 1950s, it was apparent that the bridge was not up to the rigors of the increased traffic of a quickly grow-ing Sarasota. The original ornate cement railings had long since broken off and had been replaced with wood, and the thumping of car tires over the cross beams did not instill confidence. Too, there was the errant fisherman who backed into traffic or got his hook attached to someone's bumper, or worse, hit the overhead power lines with a metal leader. Zap! (LaHurd, *Sarasota Herald-Tribune*, July 31, 2008)

It was also during this period that St. Armands also started to suffer. "Gradually, the wooden causeway began to rot, the Circle bandstand sagged, and the native vegetation covered the care-fully planned streets and sidewalks," observed the St. Armands Circle Association website. Like Rip Van Winkle, the fabulous vision activated by one of the greatest showmen on Earth slept for almost 20 years. "Children played ball where the bandstand once stood and only curious tourists ventured out to view the once-famous key. During the 1940s, several courageous investors opened restaurants and a service station on the Circle but not until 1953 did business once again resume."

In 1959, the original bridge was demolished and replaced with a four-lane drawbridge. When that proved to be inadequate to handle the increasing volume of car and marine traffic, it was again replaced in 2003 with what stands today: the 3,097-foot-long, 107-foot-wide drawbridge-less John Ringling Causeway, with its breathtaking views of sparkling Sarasota Bay, favored by bicyclers, hikers, and joggers. "With four lanes for traffic, emergency, and bicycle lanes, plus sidewalks, [it] is able to serve all types of users, and with a clearance of 60 feet, marine traffic can easily pass," noted the Florida Department of Transportation.

Ritz-Carlton

While John Ringling was big on "putting on the Ritz," even he couldn't quite pull this one off. Although in 1926, when construction began in mid-March—with an ambitious completion deadline of nine months—along with his own funds, he was gathering investors for what would become his pet project and obsession, according to Weeks, to "promote Sarasota as a rival to Miami or Palm Beach as a resort for the chic, cosmopolitan set."

John, Mable, and Ritz-Carlton President Albert Keller (far right) scout for hotel sites in 1921.
THE JOHN AND MABLE RINGLING MUSEUM OF ART ARCHIVES, PAPERS OF JOHN RINGLING, COLLECTION OF RINGLING FAMILY PHOTOGRAPHIC ALBUMS

However, as Weeks also noted, John Ringling wasn't exactly kosher when it came to his business practices, "following a convoluted course, one that might conceal the trail of assets and ownership from prying examiners or creditors" and that would, as time went on, "bec[o]me almost an obsession" and contribute to his eventual downfall and bankruptcy, including a lawsuit with his former partner and business associate Owen Burns, which played out in a courtroom in 1930.

The handwriting on the wall quickly became visible. As the hotel, located at the south end of Longboat Key, was being built and investors were being courted, the stock market began to destabilize. By fall 1926, after a hurricane devastated Miami, land values in Florida had tanked, and John Ringling ran out of funds for the hotel. According to the 1953 *Key Notes*, a now-defunct local publication, "the first of three 350 room units . . . was nearly completed after seven months of work. The first [of three planned] 18-hole golf course[s] was finished," with the necessary connecting roadwork halfway accomplished. (Actually, the number of units planned was 250.) "Sixty days more and Sarasota would have had the finest hotel in Florida." While a bit of hyperbole was involved, the Ringlings truly wanted to see the hotel come to fruition. In 1937, a year after John's death, nephews John and Henry Ringling North pledged $2 million to finish the hotel.

However, the financing never materialized, and it was left to rest in peace until early 1964, when the five-story, concrete behemoth was finally demolished. However, like rock and roll, which allegedly never dies, in 2001 the Ritz-Carlton built a hotel on the site of the old Vernona, an iconic historical loop, back to former owner Burns and John Ringling, who renamed it the Ringling Towers, where it was eventually converted to apartments and then knocked down to make way for this 21st-century Ritz whose "unparalleled luxury and experiences" allow "exclusive access to The Beach Club on Lido Key, an onsite spa, championship golf, spacious suites and guest rooms and 60,000 square feet of indoor and outdoor event space at this Gulf Coast destination," according to the hotel website.

Oh, what a tangled web. . . . Charles's death on December 3, 1926, marked a huge sea change for John Ringling. While Sarasota mourned by flying flags at half-mast and closing businesses, government offices, and banks, John had truly become the one and only "circus king."

> Despite his great energy and abilities, the demands of his other ventures, added to his sole control of the circus, presented a formidable combination. He responded by increasing his reliance on hired managers to head the circus. He could not have known that a carefully contrived tax fraud had been in progress for several years and was to continue within the circus until it was exposed nearly a decade later after a two-year federal investigation. By then nearly $4 million had disappeared. Such unscrupulous conduct, alien to the Ringling ethic, was one of the hazards of absentee ownership. (Weeks, *Ringling: The Florida Years*, 135–36)

Perhaps more importantly, he was the last of the seven brothers left alive. While this must have been devastating, "probably only Mable and their sister, Ida, knew the true state of [their] relationship," continued Weeks. But according to Plowden, even the normally undemonstrative John wept and proclaimed, "I'm the only one left."

As anyone who has ever been king—including Elvis—knows, the burden of the crown can be crushing.

Chapter 8

Ca' d' Zan

FROM "CAMELOT" TO (NOT QUITE) A PARKING LOT

–

Ca' d'Zan (n): a. Where the Doges Palace in Venice and the Gilded Age in America collide to create a stunning, over-the-(big)top explosion of art, décor, and architectural design. b. Literal meaning, "House of John" but is actually more like the House of Mable. c. Where, in discussing the donation and renovation of the Ringling home and art collection to the State of Florida—including four priceless giant tapestries from the famous Dutch artist Peter Rubens—one legislator quipped, "the only good Rubens is a sandwich." More likely, only in Florida.

If anything personifies the rags-to-riches-to-nearly-rags-again journey of John Ringling, it would be the greatest showplace in Sarasota, a five-story, 36,000-square-foot, $1.5 million behemoth with 41 rooms and 15 bathrooms. While the actual building cost would be about 22 million in today's dollars, the furnishings, art, and other embellishments make it essentially priceless. Ca' d'Zan:

> Set the stage for the area's most glamorous, most Gatsbyesque moments . . . as guests of John Ringling and his wife, Mable—New York politicians, Hollywood stars, as many as 500 people at a time—danced in the high-ceilinged court, spilling outside onto the 13,000-square-foot, all-marble terrace abutting Sarasota Bay, the music being played by a band on the deck of his yacht, the sounds drifting out onto the water and over toward the keys, most of which he owned as well. (*Sarasota* magazine)

All aboard for good times with John and Mable and their family and many friends.
THE JOHN AND MABLE RINGLING MUSEUM OF ART ARCHIVES, PAPERS OF JOHN RING-LING, COLLECTION OF RINGLING FAMILY PHOTOGRAPHIC ALBUMS

According to some sources, that would have been the *Zalophus*, although others claim that only the smaller *Zalophus, Jr.*, would have fit. Regardless, during the house's heyday, the bay-facing side also featured a gondola, just in case visitors might miss the cultural reference. Never mind that hurricane-force winds would take out the gondola; in 1930, after hitting an object about a mile off Lido Key and being battered by heavy seas, the original *Zalophus* sank in 12 feet of water.

CAMELOT, GATSBY, AND BRIGADOON

Completed in 1926, Ca' d'Zan was lived in for only three years by the Ringlings as a couple until Mable's untimely death at age 54 from diabetes, Addison's disease, and other medical issues. John remained in their winter home, although a few months after her

June 8 passing, in October 1929, the stock market crashed, decimating his fortunes and bringing to light a scandal that eventually cost him the circus and other assets. Among his many personal problems was an impulsive, disastrous second marriage that precipitated his declining health and culminated in his 1936 passing, leaving the mansion under the stewardship of the State of Florida. It's a good thing that it was solidly built since "by the late 90's, Ca' d'Zan was in such a state of disrepair it was used as the location for Miss Havisham's decrepit mansion in the . . . Hollywood remake of Charles Dickens' classic *Great Expectations*," added the Ringling Museum website.

But in 1923, "when the Ringlings had just returned from Italy (where they had acquired a great many sculptures and other objects of art as a result of their new impulse toward collecting), Mrs. Ringling announced that she intended to build a palatial home," according to "The House That John and Mable Ringling Built: A Short Guide to the Ringling Residence," a booklet published by the Ringling Museum. "Her husband, it became evident, would be satisfied with 'just a little bit of a place' but she wanted something more magnificent to be built in the style of Venice, the city that they both loved."

Mable was also packing "all manner of photographs and brochures and sketches she had commissioned from Italian artists," continued the booklet. "She had already made up her mind that she wanted something richly ornate." The architecture is often described as Venetian Gothic, a colloquial term for a "building style that combined the Gothic lancet arch with Byzantine and Ottoman influences," according to the Venice tourism website.

So it was no surprise that "Mable supervised every aspect of the building, down to the mixing of the terra cotta and the glazing of the tiles," noted the Ringling Museum website. This also extended to the design and layout of the gardens and extraction via gun or other means of the various wild critters that resided there.

Mable's Gardens: Green Gifts
That Keep on Giving

Mable's gardening efforts still blossom in Sarasota today. "Mable envisioned an estate with exotic trees and plants and collected them with the same passion that her husband collected art," observed the Ringling website. The first was in 1913, at what eventually became the 27,225-square-foot, Italian-inspired Rose Garden. Located in the 66-acre Ringling compound, "its circular design [is] patterned after a wagon wheel, its pathways lined with garden sculptures."

Silhouetted against the beauty of the bay, this Ringling-era statue offers an interesting, if rather tacky, study in contrast.
SANDRA GURVIS

In contrast to the breathtakingly gorgeous trees, plants, and flowers, these crepuscular-tinged statues of courting couples—along with elves and other Hobbit-esque creatures in the nearby Dwarf Garden—are mausoleum grade and borderline freak show. (John also picked out some of the statuary, which explains a lot.)

Mable's endeavors were recognized and appreciated by the community: Along with being elected as the first president of the Sarasota Garden Club in 1927, a year later (shortly before her 1929 death), she was made director of the Sarasota Women's Club. In the mid-1930s, a fountain and reflecting pool in Luke Wood Park, near downtown Sarasota, were installed as a memorial to her and restored in her honor in 2014 by the Garden Club.

Actually, the Bayfront Gardens, as they are called today, encompass much more than Mable's Rose, Secret, and Dwarf gardens. In fact, with over 2,350 "native, exotic, historical, and culturally significant" trees, according to the Ringling website, the complex's 66 acres are designated as a Level II arboretum by ArbNet, the international arboretum accrediting organization. But perhaps more important to visitors, they provide a welcome respite from Florida's blazing sun.

Other prized shady spots are the Millennium Tree Trail, created to mark the year 2000, which connects via the even newer (2010) Bolger Bayfront Promenade and Campiello (small square) to Ca' d'Zan. So visitors can pretend they are John Ringling surveying their "kingdom" overlooking the Bay . . . for a moment at least. The U-shaped courtyard is also included as part of the gardens, although it's primarily Classical, Renaissance, and Baroque statuary and a moat, with some juniper and slash pine trees.

Mable's green, otherworldly touch can also be found in the Secret Garden, where she, John, and John's sister, Ida, were also eventually planted. "Mable created this garden with plants given to her by friends and neighbors during her winters at Ca' d'Zan," the website notes. "She enjoyed entertaining her guests by taking them on tours." In a sense she continues to do so.

NO SIMPLE MOVE

With this in mind and with a seemingly bottomless pocketbook, the Ringlings—or rather, Mable—went about organizing the move of their comparatively humble frame clapboard abode to another part of the property, where it was eventually torn down, and acquired two smaller parcels, enlarging the land devoted to the estate to about 36 acres. The entire complex, which today includes the Museum of Art, Circus Museum, Asolo Theater, Education Center, gardens, and other adjacent buildings, is around 60 acres.

The Ringlings interviewed several architects until deciding on Dwight James Baum of New York, although he and Mable often clashed as—again, not unexpectedly—"she demanded many changes to his plans," noted Aaron De Groft and David Weeks in *Ca' d'Zan: Inside the Ringling Mansion*. A former director of the Ringling Museum of Art, De Groft was also instrumental in helping to save, restore, and renovate Ca' d'Zan in the late 1990s and early 2000s.

Baum himself was a bit of a prima donna. He was "never certain that Ca' d'Zan was more than a capricious, even fantastic eccentricity," observed De Groft and Weeks. The "conflict between the design and the Florida location" along with Mable's capriciousness resulted in Baum's decision to revise "the terms of his agreement from a fixed fee to one based on time and materials."

Among the major sticking points was Mable's desire to replicate part of the "old" Madison Square Garden (MSG), an ornate Beaux Arts–style confection with a Baroque tower estimated to be some 32 stories high. Designed in 1890 by famous architect Stanford White, a notorious womanizer who had been murdered there by a jealous husband, an earlier iteration of MSG had been constructed in 1874 by none other than P. T. Barnum. Aside from its obvious connection with both circuses, which played there many times, John's involvement with MSG—he was also part owner—allowed him to rub shoulders or at least claim an association with New York City luminaries whose last names included Morgan,

Beset by constantly changing specifications and deadlines, construction of Ca' d'Zan was a challenge to say the least.
THE JOHN AND MABLE RINGLING MUSEUM OF ART ARCHIVES, WOODILL ALBUM

Vanderbilt, and Astor. These folk tended to look down at John, who was still referred to as a former clown and circus performer in the press and elsewhere. But John was determined to make his mark.

> Working with his longtime associate Tex Rickard, [John] was helping to put together a scheme for a new sports arena in New York City. The team acquired for $2 million a site on Eighth Avenue between 49th and 50th streets. There they would build the new Madison Square Garden, the largest building in the world devoted exclusively to entertainment. The new Garden opened in late 1926. Ringling continued as chairman and Tex Rickard as president. (Weeks, *Ringling: The Florida Years*, 118)

Although the Ca' d'Zan tower was supposed to mimic Madison Square Garden, the end product was quite different. As was the view.

While smaller and limited to the bay-facing side, Ca' d'Zan's take on MSG only bears a passing resemblance. Despite the fact that Baum and associates spent months struggling to meet Mable's specifications, John nixed their plans, claiming it would be too costly. Ca' d'Zan does have a tower, of course, an approximately five-story testament to John's success, where "not only the light in [its] loggia was seen from afar, but also it was believed that with all of the doors to the Great Hall open during parties the great . . . organ could be heard across Sarasota Bay to Longboat Key," noted De Groft in his thesis, "John Ringling in *Perpetua Memoria*: The Legacy and Prestige of Art and Collecting."

SO MANY FEATURES, SO LITTLE TIME

Located over the dining area, the open-air tower looks down to the marbled terrace, offering glimmering hints of the lightly tinted Venetian glass in the mansion's minaret-shaped windows;

Although they are high maintenance, these stained glass windows personify the elegance of Ca' d'Zan.
SANDRA GURVIS

the 240-foot-long marble terrace; and of course, that breathtaking panorama of the bay.

The inside of the house defines eclectic. To get a full sense of the entrance and foyer, ballroom, court/living room, think circa 1990s Hyatt Regency hotel lobby but with really expensive art and fewer bedrooms. Breakfast and formal dining rooms, kitchen, and much more require intensive examination and many repeat visits. For example, along with oversized black and white "checkerboard" tiled marble floor, the court also boasts a crystal chandelier from the original Waldorf-Astoria Hotel. A few other highlights follow.

DANCING ON THE CEILING WITH WILLY POGANY

While people today may be unfamiliar with the Hungarian-born artist Willy Pogany (1882–1955), back then he was a big deal, with his art nouveau illustrations appearing in everything from children's books to museum walls to stage and movie sets. Mable came up with idea of having Pogany paint his whimsical figures not only on the ceiling of the ballroom but also on the third-floor game room. The ballroom array, somewhat pretentiously titled *Dance of the Nations*, features panels of 22 dancing couples set amid gilded octagons. While some may be politically or historically incorrect by today's standards, Pogany, who created the works in his New York studio rather than from a ladder à la Michelangelo, "once commented that all the figures, no matter how diverse, were moving to the same rhythm," noted De Groft and Weeks. This also applies to a fantastical panel featuring female nudity, inadvertently designed to engage the interest of teenage boys who might otherwise be uninterested in the tour. The less formal game room ceiling depicts a Venetian carnival with a younger John and Mable as the centerpiece, surrounded by a menagerie of their pets, including John's favorite German Shepherd, Tel, and Mable's ill-tempered cockatoo, Laura, and a self-portrait of the artist wielding a dripping paintbrush.

Dancing on the ceiling with John, Mable, and their pets.
SANDRA GURVIS

THAT CRAZY BEDROOM ARRANGEMENT

This setup could be a cross between *The Real Housewives* and *Big Brother*. Imagine being the second wife having to go through the dead first wife's luxe bedroom to spend time with hubby, plus being surrounded by all the stuff picked out by Wife No. 1. Add to the mix the Depression, bills piling up, and hubby refusing to sell even a single piece of art from his museum to stave off creditors asking you for a loan instead. These were among the problems facing Emily Haag Buck, who married John Ringling a mere year and a half after Mable passed away.

Far less ornate than John's or Mable's, the "second Mrs. Ringling's bedroom" is only mentioned in passing in the 1951 museum booklet and not at all in De Groft and Weeks's publication over 50 years later. In contrast, John's bedroom reflects his ostentatious life choices: "decorated in French Empire style, with gilded enframements of doors and windows," noted the Ringling Museum booklet. "On its ceiling is an oval painted decoration," *Dawn Drives Away Darkness*, of angels and chariots from the late-19th-century artist Jacob de Wit. "The suite of furniture, in the revived Empire style of Napoleon III, is of rosewood, heavily encrusted with gilded bronze ornamentation." And so on.

But what really stands out is that the beds are short (they are, after all, named after Napoleon), whereas John was a strapping 6 foot 4 inches by some accounts. Equally as fascinating are an agglomeration of his "big and tall" shirts and pants and trademark boater hats hanging in the closet. With the gold-plated fixtures and marble bathtub carved from a six-foot cube, John's Siena marble–walled bathroom arguably rivals a certain insurrection-minded former president. Not as ostentatious but equally impressive, Mable's spacious bedroom/dressing room combo consists of gilded, marble-topped rococo Louis IV–style furniture and gorgeous fabrics and tapestries on the walls and elsewhere, making it as desirable a living space today as it was back then.

A peek inside John's closet reveals much about the man.
SANDRA GURVIS

PECKY CYPRESS AND THE GAME ROOM

The holes in this relatively rare type of wood are caused by a fungus, rather than Woody Woodpecker. Yet the end result of what essentially is "a brown pocket rot," according to the What Is Pecky Cypress and More website, and is not only distinctive and durable but relatively rare these days and expensive. Pecky cypress provides support for two of the mansion's biggest rooms—the court and game room—and represents one of the few uses of wood in a house solidly constructed from terra cotta "T" blocks, concrete, and masonry, designed to stand up to sea air, storms, and Florida heat. The playroom, originally intended to be an attic, ended up as an adult-sized "Pee-wee's playhouse" with a card and pool table, oversized chairs, and a gramophone, among other items.

JOHN'S GIANT ORGAN, "EXERCISE ROOM," AND VAULT

While not immediately visible to today's visitors, during the Ringling years the 2,250-plus pipe Aeolian organ was "prominently displayed in the grand court . . . to provide background music during their intimate dinner parties" as well as "large garden parties and musicales featuring guest artists who came from New York, Boston and Tampa" to play it, according to the Ringling website. Although silent for decades, it is in the process of being restored to its previous resounding musical glory thanks to a $1.5 million grant from the Wyncote Foundation and individual donations, potentially adding an auditory element to the already visual overstimulation.

With a massage table and vibrating-belt "weight loss" machine, the so-called exercise room was in name only. Although it's on a different floor than John's taproom, whose highlight is a brass-railed bar from his favorite St. Louis restaurant, the vault—ostensibly built to store the Ringlings' jewelry and other valuables—also hid John's "own private stock of bourbon along with bottles upon bottles of champagne and beer and absinthe and vermouth and whatever else anybody visiting could have desired," notes *Sarasota* magazine. While "Prohibition was in full effect, wealthy people like the Ringlings were still well supplied with wine and spirits," states the Ringling site. No stills and "revenuers" for these folks.

NOT CLOSE ENOUGH FOR GOVERNMENT WORK

"There are few sights sadder than a grand old house fallen on hard times—unkempt, unloved and utterly forlorn," observed *Architectural Digest*. "For six full decades, from John Ringling's death in 1936 until 1996, that was the fate of Ca' d'Zan," as well as the rest of the museum complex.

Although John left a $1.2 million endowment to care for the property, "over the years the money sat in state coffers and

Although Ca' d'Zan did fall into disrepair, it still looked pretty good from a distance.
THE JOHN AND MABLE RINGLING MUSEUM OF ART ARCHIVES COLLECTION OF PHOTOGRAPHS

the house slowly deteriorated from the elements and the steady stream of visitors," according to an account in the *South Florida Sun-Sentinel*. By 2000, the endowment had grown to less than $1.8 million. "Under a mattress it would have done better than that," John Wetenhall, former executive director of the John and Mable Ringling Museum of Art, semi-jokingly told the paper.

"Poor Ringling!" lamented *Architectural Digest*. "His magnificent gift was all but spat upon." Although Ca' d'Zan was opened to the public in 1946, upkeep was patchwork at best. Left to the whims of indifferent state legislators, "deferred maintenance," so called by De Groft and Weeks, resulted in faded fabrics, leaky roofs, collapsed railings, and more and a terrace "in such disrepair that it was dangerous for visitors to even walk upon it." The "once sparkling palace" had deteriorated into a "decrepit ruin." What few restorations had taken place "had been repeatedly altered and changed so that the entirety no longer reflected original taste."

In 1996, a six-year, $15 million restoration began, and the mansion was closed for three years. "Layers of wall paint were examined to determine each original color, while vintage photographs and written accounts were studied to measure historical accuracy," continued De Groft and Weeks.

Among the photos were an eBay "find" of pictures of the original construction, which greatly helped with the re-creation of the exterior. "Next came the interior and the meticulous restoration of all those items found in the bat-infested attic and the art museum's dank basement," noted *Architectural Digest*, not to mention the birds, roaches, and other critters that had decided to take up residence in the house and grounds. Things had been placed higgledy-piggledy, and it took a small army of curators, researchers, and restorers to figure out what was supposed to go where.

According to the *Sun-Sentinel*, "curators drew on craftsmen and artisans around the world to repair the tapestries, clean the painted ceilings and re-create what couldn't be salvaged. Among the triumphs of the restoration are two Louis XIV–style chairs the Ringlings bought from the Astor family. Both had become ratty." With regard to the tapestries, "each day, several volunteers from the Embroiders Guild of America and the American Needlepoint Guild arrived to quietly work on re-creating the original colors and stitching." Additional updates included the installation of modern climate control, fire protection, and security systems.

"In 2000, governance of the Ringling Museum was transferred from Florida's Department of State to Florida State University and a new board of directors was appointed to see the restoration to completion," stated De Groft and Weeks. And two years later, Ca' d'Zan "reopened to record crowds," although renovations of the grand old flapper continue to this day.

If Ca' d'Zan has a lesson it might be this:

Although it's impeccably restored, Ca' d'Zan today remains a continual home improvement project.
SANDRA GURVIS

For a time, John and Mable Ringling had nearly everything they wanted. From the beginning, the house was
indeed a showcase-unrivaled and unique in Sarasota, with
public rooms that served as venues to display the many
Ringling treasures brought from Europe or purchased at
New York auctions. . . . Ca' d'Zan continues to embody
the lasting monument of the lives of John and Mable. . .
. [It] remains a preeminent jewel . . . and stands out as a
signature of the great legacy of fine art and culture that the
Ringlings envisioned on the shores of Sarasota Bay. (De
Groft and Weeks, *Ca' d'Zan: Inside the Ringling*, 63–64)

That is, once the powers that be decided it was worth
preserving.

Chapter 9

The Museum

THE ART "HOUSE OF JOHN"

In 1925, when John Ringling announced his intention to build an art museum, he was at the height of his influence and was considered to be one of the richest men in the world. But he was also "an aesthete, a self-taught art connoisseur and collector" according to Florida State University, which oversees the museum today. To achieve this end, Ringling befriended Julius "LuLu" Böhler, a renowned German art dealer, who served as his wing man, helping John obtain the desired acquisitions at the best possible price. Because if the circus had taught John Ringling anything, it was to avoid being perceived as a punter with greenbacks hanging from his pockets. Not to mention steering around what might have resulted in a clown car full of bad taste.

Ringling also enlisted architect John H. Phillips, designer of New York City's Metropolitan Museum of Art and Grand Central Terminal, to create the 21-gallery museum with its U-shaped wraparound courtyard and stunning, albeit slightly far-off, view of Sarasota Bay, all the better to help keep its treasures safe from storm/hurricane damage. Modeled after the circa 1560 Uffizi Gallery in Florence, Italy, it represents an economy of space and beauty, shot through with trademark Ringling glitz.

"[John's] vision for the collection was to build an art museum in Sarasota . . . to establish the burgeoning city as a cultural and educational center," noted the Florida State University website. But it was only the first step in what would become a magnet for both the arts and tourism.

John Ringling in his prime. He didn't smile much, but here he had a lot to smile about.

A LULU OF A COLLABORATION

John and Mable befriended LuLu and his wife in the early 1920s. At that time John was purchasing items that according to David Weeks in *Ringling: The Florida Years*, "he believed would convey an air of elegance and upper-class taste," for the planned Sarasota Ritz-Carlton. Many of these acquisitions ended up in the museum and in their various residences, including the storage areas of Ca' d'Zan, which eventually became a treasure trove of forgotten relics.

The Ringling/Böhler combo resulted in the procurement of over 400 paintings and thousands of objects d'art. Their collaboration was a rarity in the art world since at that time agents usually made buying decisions independently for their rich clients. In an essay written in 1948, "Böhler related that once Ringling had decided to build a museum, he purchased and studied many books on art and 'became very quickly not only enthusiastic but quite a good judge of pictures,'" noted Eric Zafran in *John Ringling: Dreamer, Builder, Collector*. As time went on, Ringling occasionally even overruled his teacher.

Böhler's pedigree helped seal the many deals. "Böhler was greatly respected . . . in Munich, the owner of a first-rank collection and a palatial gallery," stated Weeks. Although Böhler had other clients, he "was a true friend in the sense that he understood Ringling's position . . . that [Ringling] wished to assemble a large collection to fill his museum and that he wished to do so speedily and in a certain price range." Along helping sniff out good quality at a reasonable cost, Böhler also exhibited a "genuineness [and] was never arrogant."

In addition to amassing an extravaganza of Renaissance and Baroque artists such as Cranach, Velasquez, Piero di Cosimo, Veronese, Titian, Poussin, and Frans Hals, the Ringling/Böhler combo acquired "statues, columns, marble doorways and bronzes" from the Chiurazzi foundry in Italy, which was noted for its reproduction of classic works. While also originally intended for the Ritz-Carlton, several statues of the Classical, Renaissance, and

"David" then and now. As these photos illustrate, not much has changed.
TIBBALS CIRCUS COLLECTION OF POSTCARDS AND SANDRA GURVIS.

Baroque persuasion were instead placed in the courtyard, including the showstopper, an almost 17-foot, anatomically correct bronze cast of Michelangelo's "David."

CARTOONS BUT NOT COMIC STRIPS

John made his bones as a serious art collector in 1926. Among the most dramatic of that year's purchases and the first thing most museum visitors see is an eye-popping display of four ginormous "cartoons" from Dutch painter Peter Paul Rubens (1577–1640). These "cartoons" are actually masterpieces, part of the "Triumph of the Eucharist" series and the only large-scale Rubens paintings outside of Europe.

> Rubens intended [them] to serve as models for a succession of tapestries for the Archduchess Isabella Eugenia, the Governess of the Netherlands and the sister of the King of Spain. Of the remaining tapestries, two are held in the

Louvre in Paris, four were lost to fire, and one was owned by a private party in England since 1842. The last, obtained by the Ringling Museum in 1980, was unveiled to the public in celebration of the institution's 50th birthday. (Amanda Ellen Meter, *John Ringling: Story of a Capitalist*, 31)

Each ornately housed and framed "cartoon" tells a story.

The Meeting of Abraham and Melchizedek
While depicting an episode from Genesis 14:17-24 (Abraham's victorious return from the battle of Dan), this more resembles an entire season of *Survivor*, Old Testament edition. The plot is simple, however; Abraham is being blessed by the priest Melchizedek, who offers him bread and wine, while a cluster of acolytes assists. Well perhaps not all; the guy at the bottom right looks like he's plotting something nefarious—just like in *Survivor*.

The Gathering of the Manna
It's Passover's first cousin: Taken from Exodus 16:13-36, this portrait "represents a second miraculous feeding . . . of the Israelites during their journey through the Sinai desert," according to the museum website. "The white flakes of Manna that mysteriously fell from Heaven are . . . shown as round wafers that resemble the host of the Mass." Or perhaps it was the Jewish flatbread known as Matzah since the exodus took place about 1,200 years or so before Jesus was born.

The Four Evangelists
Although this portrays the very serious subject of the Last Supper, it could also resemble an ancient album cover for a singing group of the same name. Of course, it's already taken by Sts. Matthew, Mark, Luke, and John. The gesturing angel, the backside of an ox, and John, eyes and goblet cast heavenward like he's giving it all he's got, add that touch of rock and roll.

Paintings such as The Gathering of the Manna offer glimpses of human suffering without the modern conveniences.
SANDRA GURVIS

The Defenders of the Eucharist

These Catholic priests look like they would rather be anywhere but in this portrait. Especially Jerome, clad in red, who has his nose buried in the Bible—understandable since he is about to get last rites. But replace that book with a cell phone, and he could also be zoning out on a video game.

Despite being a quick study himself, with a lifelong passion for design that originated with the now-iconic circus posters, John had been considered somewhat of a comic strip character in the art world. However, after he started dropping serious cash, he became more of a clown prince, with even the snootiest auction dealers referring to him as "Mr. Ringling."

Between 1925 and 1931, Ringling acquired more than 600 Old Master paintings from the Late Medieval through the 19th century. . . . In 1928, Ringling made another significant acquisition that was to form the core of his classical antiquities collection, 2800 objects of Greek, Roman, and Cypriot antiquities from the Metropolitan Museum of Art in New York. Excitement about his collection was growing in art circles; *The New York Times* did a full-page article about the purchase, praising not only the collection but the Museum and its surroundings as well. That same year he bought the Parisian Gavet Collection, 300 hundred pieces of Late Medieval and Early Renaissance decorative art, sculpture and religious liturgical objects from the Vanderbilt's Marble House in Newport, Rhode Island. (Ringling museum website)

Including post–Ringling era acquisitions, today the museum houses a mind-boggling total of "more than 28,000 works that represent Western and non-Western art from ancient periods, the European Middle Ages to the nineteenth century, and American art of the twentieth and twenty-first centuries," continued the museum website.

Several of the museum's galleries are fronted by a shotgun array of twisted Solomonic columns, a design element favored by John's buddy, architect Stanford White. They provide a dramatic setting for not only the paintings but also jewelry, ceramics, sculptures, and other media. Groupings are by artists and/or period, with the exquisite oddity, such as a circa 1600s miniature ebony and tortoiseshell cabinet with painted panels.

Even those less inclined to spend hours or even days perusing the various objects d'art might pause at the Astor Crème Salon and the Astor Library. They represent a grand finale of a sort and as with any performance, are guaranteed crowd pleasers. Ringling also purchased these in 1926, from—surprise!—the Astor mansion in New York City, which was slated for demolition that same year. The mansion was built in the mid-1890s for Mrs. William

Where's Rembrandt? Try to find your favorite artist in this elegant hodge-podge of good taste.
SANDRA GURVIS

Backhouse Astor, aka Caroline Schermerhorn Astor, and her son, Col. John Jacob Astor IV by the Gilded Age architect Richard Morris Hunt.

Ma Astor's circle of influence melded nicely with the Ringling desire for cache.

[She] was perhaps the most powerful social lioness America has ever known. With her family's social rank and the Astor fabulous wealth [she] made late nineteenth century New York society into her personal domain and repulsed every challenge to her position as its ruling queen. Her control over admission to New York's highest social circles was enforced through the adroit manipulation of the guest lists to her famous parties. By extending or withholding the coveted invitations, Mrs. Astor was able to chastise the social misdemeanors of her friends even as she stifled the bolder encroachments of the *nouveaux riche*. Her task was made easier by the limited size of her ballroom, which could comfortably accommodate no more than four hundred guests. That "Four Hundred" . . . came to define New York society in the last decades of the nineteenth century. (Michael Conforti, *John Ringling: Dreamer, Builder, Collector*, 127)

A heck of a place to throw a party—the Astor Crème Salon.
SANDRA GURVIS

The white and gold gilded French rococo explosion of mirrors and candelabras fronted by an elaborate marble fireplace make it easy to visualize Ma Astor's dressed to impress "400" as they sashayed about, attempting to ape their more pedigreed European ancestors. In direct contrast, the spacious Regency-style oak-paneled library was originally a dining room before John Jacob duded it into an extremely large turn-of-the-20th-century man cave, where he and the other mustachioed and tuxedoed bros sat around smoking cigars and indulging in adult beverages with high alcoholic content.

EARLY DAZE: THE STRUGGLE WAS REAL

The creation and organization of the museum and its early years were challenging, to say the least. "The property, much of which was under water, contained . . . rattlesnakes, copperheads, and alligators," observed Aaron De Groft in his thesis, "John Ringling in *Perpetua Memoria*: The Legacy and Prestige of Art and Collecting." To create level ground on which to build, some areas had to be drained and refilled with solid material."

The construction, which began in June 1927, turned out to be a bit of a mishmash. John hired a buddy, Lyman Chase, and skilled laborers from his circus—two-footed, not four—after the first firm, Hageman and Harris of Tampa, proved too pricey. By that time, the circus winter headquarters had conveniently moved from Bridgeport, Connecticut, to Sarasota. John was also encountering financial issues, including the failing Ritz-Carlton project. So he cut other corners, such as eliminating some insulation in the walls, which eventually produced dampness and separation, a problem not completely fixed until the 1990 renovation, and alterations in the construction of the roof, "resulting in a great deal of leakage," which plagued the museum for decades," observed De Groft.

Additional adjustments included "abandoning a plan for a large extension of the north wing beyond the picture galleries to house a school of art and student dormitories," noted Weeks. "Both John and Mable were committed to forming a school and only reluctantly accepted the fact that they did not have the money." As things grew more difficult and finances even tighter, John refused to sell a single piece of art, despite the pleas of second wife, Emily Haag Buck, and his bankers.

The museum premiered—for one day—on March 31, 1930, "allowing the public and Ringling's guests to view his entire collection for the first time," stated Meter. "[T]he paintings were specially arranged in triple-hung salon style, allowing visitors to see in excess of 500 works at once, a figure more than double what is traditionally on display now."

After a couple of false starts, the museum opened again to the public in March 1931, this time to large crowds and a full-page spread in *The New York Times*. "The John and Mable

Historical aerial photo of Ringling Museum, B.D. (Before Developers).
THE JOHN AND MABLE RINGLING MUSEUM OF ART ARCHIVES COLLECTION OF PHOTOGRAPHS

Ringling Museum was proclaimed to house the finest collection in the South, set within an architectural framework reminiscent of those by [such] collector-barons . . . as J.P. Morgan and Henry Clay Frick," writes Heather Ewing in *John Ringling: Dreamer, Builder, Collector*. Raved the *New York World*, "On the northern edge of this little Florida town, John Ringling, who used to drive a circus wagon, has built one of the finest museums of art in all the world."

Yet until John's death in 1936 when he bequeathed it to the State of Florida, the museum was plagued with disorganization and a deficit in credibility, which included, among other things, a lack of a catalogue for its collections (important) as well as a professional administrator (even more important), although some accounts cite Julius Böhler as the first curator. It remained open until John's death in 1936, when he bequeathed it to the State of Florida.

> Hurt by the Depression, Ringling had fallen into debt and creditors and legal wrangling would delay the settling of his estate for a decade. Funds were poorly managed and the endowment Ringling left languished and barely grew. The Museum was only occasionally opened between 1936 and 1946 and not properly maintained. Gradually, the care that the buildings required were either put off or handled piecemeal. (Ringling Museum website)

Despite the hard times, litigation, leaky roofs, and crumbling edifices, John and Mable's creation of their two gemstones, Ca' d'Zan and the museum, made a huge impact on Sarasota.

> The Ringling Museum was the birthplace of many of the other cultural institutions in Sarasota today. It is widely known amongst Sarasotans that the opera, symphony and ballet all started in one fashion or another either as a result

of the cultural impetus of the museum, or the fact that the physical structure of the museum was the first venue for these fledgling institutions. Sarasota is widely viewed by Floridians, especially the cultural cognoscenti, as the cultural capital of Florida. Without John Ringling's collecting and building endeavors the sleepy fishing village may have remained just that. (De Groft, "John Ringling in *Perpetua Memoria*," 239)

Chapter 10

The Circus Comes to Town

EXPANSION OF THE RINGLING IMPRINT

The Ringling influence encompasses far more than Ca' d'Zan and John and Mable's namesake museum. In fact, it might almost be impossible to quantify every aspect of life in this region that has been touched by the family, ripples that extended as far as Gibsonton, some 50 miles north. In the 1940s, "Gibtown," as it is sometimes called, became ground zero for "freaks and geeks," aka circus and carnival performers, during their off-season. If Sarasota was spring training for the circus world "when veterans would teach the rookies . . . the tricks of their trade and secrets of tapping into human emotion," according to the Visit Sarasota website, then Gibtown was its carny equivalent. As with Sarasota, Gibtown moved on, a working-class community whose oddball past is memorialized in the International Independent Showmen's Museum.

But for a few captivating decades, Sarasota was a "circus town," which contributed to its many cultural and entertainment amenities, including the Circus Museum, the Ringling College of Art + Design, the Asolo Theater, the Ringling Educational Center, and eventually the Circus Arts Conservatory and more discussed in chapter 12. Others such as the Sarasota Art Museum, Marie Selby Gardens, and Van Wezel Performing Arts Hall came into existence as other wealthy benefactors flocked to the area.

CIRCUS CITY—FOR A WHILE, ANYWAY

For John Ringling, 1927 was a year of contradictions. On one hand, construction of the Museum of Art was finally underway. On the other, the bottom had fallen out of the Florida real estate market. "Scores of banks closed. . . . Businesses . . . went bankrupt, and people left the state in droves," observed Gene Plowden in *Those Amazing Ringlings and Their Circus*. In Sarasota, buildings that "started with tremendous fanfare stood like gaunt, bony skeletons." Streets and sidewalks began and then abruptly stopped, like unfinished sentences. "Weeds and sandspurs covered parkways and vacant lots while scraggly grass spewed up through cracks in the pavement."

Still, John acted as if he was one of the richest men around, although he was playing a shell game with various assets to keep his pet projects moving along. He embraced his role as Sarasota's

One of the few non–Ringling buildings to survive the area's economic downturns, the El Vernona Hotel was initially built by Owen Burns for his wife, Vernona, and later became the John Ringling Hotel and then the John Ringling Towers.
THE JOHN AND MABLE RINGLING MUSEUM OF ART ARCHIVES, PAPERS OF JOHN RINGLING, COLLECTION OF RINGLING FAMILY PHOTOGRAPHIC ALBUMS

savior—purchasing the radio station, helming the Bank of Sarasota, and moving his circus here from Bridgeport, Connecticut. When they weren't performing or traveling, its many skilled artisans helped construct the art museum, along with injecting much-needed money into the economy:

> Uncle John . . . foresaw that it not only would be a great tourist attraction for his beloved little city but would reduce circus overhead. The great cost of heating those block-long brick animal barns in Bridgeport would be virtually eliminated, for only the most delicate animals would need artificial heat in Florida, and then only for a short time. In addition, he thought the circus people could live far more comfortably and cheaply in Florida. (Ringling North, *The Circus Kings*, 155)

Although the Ringlings themselves did not socialize with circus folk, they did ensure that they were taken care of at the winter quarters: "an entire complex of buildings and rail lines on

Ringling built tents, not houses, for performers and others who came to Sarasota for winter quarters.
THE JOHN AND MABLE RINGLING MUSEUM OF ART ARCHIVES COLLECTION OF POSTCARDS

the transformed [Sarasota] fairgrounds" consisted of "three barns, each with stalls for 400 horses . . . as well as dormitories, shops and menagerie houses," noted Weeks in *Ringling: The Florida Years*. John "had the circus grounds made . . . attractive . . . welcoming visitors with an avenue of coconut palms leading from the entrance to the animal houses, large car shops, stables, and rail yards. And the tourists did come, as many as 3,000 . . . in one day."

40 Acres and Some "Midgets": The Houses That John Didn't Build

Now located on North Beneva Road, site of the now defunct but unrelated Circus City Trailer Park and today, the Glen Oaks subdivision, winter quarters spawned a raft of urban legends, including homes that Ringling specifically built for "little people" (previously known as midgets) and other entertainers. For example, it might be easy to extrapolate that the cozy 1920s bungalows on Burns Court in downtown Sarasota were constructed for the vertically challenged. But in reality, they were the creation of developer Owen Burns and architect Thomas Reed Martin during the land boom. And some 100 years later, the approximately 1,000-square-foot rehabbed gems are for giant-sized budgets, going for upward of $1 million.

Other diminutive residences in and around downtown Sarasota were also built in the 1920s and 1930s, possibly by and for circus folk, although specific provenances are hard to come by. Among them is a circa 1937 residence, the "Doll House," aptly named after the Doll family, four dwarf sibs who hailed from Germany and were Ringling entertainers and played Munchkins in the *Wizard of Oz*. Allegedly used by the circus for performers, this address was also supposedly the Doll's retirement dream house. It is currently available on Airbnb for Barbies and/or Kens, 55 and over optional.

In the 1950s, one Mrs. Neal Chaplin Swalm had set aside 40 acres to create "a Florida version of Munchkinland, with buildings and roads designed for people less than four feet tall," according to the *Bradenton Times*, joining the ranks of other "midget cities" throughout the United States and abroad. In addition to being "a spectacle for tourists who would be renting rooms at a nearby 'normal sized' hotel . . . the miniature people would bring miniature fruit to sell to guests when they arrived on the bus." Along with free rent, Swalm would provide housing, lodging, and infrastructure with public services to include a mayor/police/fire department. The only thing this Tiny Town overlord asked was that its denizens pay utilities and "run . . . the businesses that she would build onsite." Her biggest moneymaker: "television publicity and a small-scale girls fashion industry where children could buy 'ladies' clothing' that resembled there [*sic*] mothers' attire." The plan never came to fruition, for reasons lost to history but are fairly obvious (civil rights, feminism, etc.).

Anita Bartholomew, a freelance journalist who resided in Sarasota in the early 2000s, purchased and rehabbed another charming cottage, even writing a book, *The Midget's House: A Circus Story . . . A Love Story . . . A Ghost Story*. But it was just that—a story—although the house is purportedly haunted. "The legend about midgets living in this house is not based on any truth that I could find," Bartholomew told the *Sarasota Herald-Tribune*.

Yet it still persists, despite a disclaimer by none other than John Ringling's grandniece, Pat Ringling Buck. "Ringling myths are in great supply in Sarasota, and over the years any number of properties have been misidentified as built by John Ringling," she stated in the *Herald-Tribune*. "The fact is that John Ringling built Ca' d'Zan and his museum. He did not build homes for his friends or for his employees." And that's as close to the horse's mouth as one can get these days.

While the clowns, lion tamers, trapeze artists, tightrope walkers, and their accompanying menagerie of, among others, lions, tigers, and bears—oh my!—may have initially been looked at askance by the locals, they soon became integrated into Sarasota's already somewhat quirky culture.

> During the next 33 years there were bits and pieces of the circus scattered throughout the city: backyard riggings for the aerialists, Circus Day Sales, circus themes and performances in restaurants like Casa Canastrelli's and the John Ringling Hotel, circus benefits for St. Martha's Church, circus parades associated with the annual Sara de Sota Pageant, the Circus Hall of Fame, circus performers as classmates and neighbors, the blessing of the circus trains by Father (later Monsignor) Elslander . . . and news accounts of the circus as it traveled throughout the country. (Jeff LaHurd, *Sarasota Herald-Tribune*)

By 1960, however, the circus had suffered many setbacks, including a horrific 1944 fire in Hartford, Connecticut, that claimed 167 lives and at the time was believed to be due to circus malfeasance but later revealed to be the result of arson. John Ringling North, Ida's son and John Ringling's nephew, still managed the circus, although in 1957, he:

> entered into an agreement with concert promoter Irvin Feld, under which the circus continued performing—not under the big-top tent but in indoor facilities which Feld contracted. Without the need to put up and take down the tent, the circus was able to reduce costs and cut its workforce from about 1,400 to about 300 individuals (including some 80 performers). (Britannica.com)

As a result, winter quarters moved up the road near the Venice airport since it no longer needed the acreage but did require a railroad connection. It stayed there for 32 years, until 1992, when the Seminole Gulf Railroad abandoned the deteriorating tracks.

The circus again relocated to the Florida State Fairgrounds in Tampa, where it remained until 2014, when it returned closer to its Sarasota roots, settling about 20 miles north into its current headquarters in Ellenton. By then, however, it had long passed from Ringling family hands:

> In late 1967, Irvin and Israel Feld and Judge Roy Hofheinz, along with capital from Richard C. Blum bought the company from the Ringling family. Hofheinz was the founder of the Houston Colt 45s . . . and . . . built the Astrodome. In 1971, the circus was sold to the Mattel Corp. for $40 million, but the Feld family continued to manage it. Irvin Feld died in 1984 and the company has since been run by Kenneth Feld. (Weeklies, *Akron Beacon Journal*)

But Sarasota did not exit gently from its role as "Circus City."

> The Ringling management of recent years has operated in a far different vein than did the late John Ringling. They have been all out to get everything possible for the circus. They didn't generate kind feelings in many instances, including the sale of the Winter Quarters land which had been obtained without cost from the county. . . . But Sarasota has also made its own place in the tourists' sun and many, many fine attractions and a wonderful climate combine to attract tourists from all over the world. (*Sarasota Herald-Tribune*)

SEND IN THE CLOWNS: THE CIRCUS MUSEUM AND CLOWN COLLEGE

Although John Ringling created neither the circus museum nor the Clown College, he would likely have supported the idea of not only educating the public as to the ways of the circus but also training its performers. And in fact, the idea for a Circus Museum, which opened in 1948, came from the Ringling Museum's first director, professional magician and Harvard graduate A. Everett "Chick" Austin Jr.

Austin, who also had quite the track record from his previous gig at the Wadsworth Atheneum Museum of Art in Hartford, Connecticut, "where he had pioneered the integration of the performing and visual arts," noted the Ringling website, had been appointed to the Ringling in 1946 at the invitation of Millard Caldwell, then Florida's governor. His initial undertaking, the Circus Museum, was the first in the United States devoted to circus history. And the plethora of costumes, fliers, props, and posters donated by local circus families provided a wealth of material for exhibits. Austin focused on the exterior as well: "To the Ringling's garage, [he] designed the addition of a rotunda, with a roof resembling a circus tent, and Corinthian pillars tying the structure's aesthetic to the Museum of Art," continued the Ringling website. Inside, it was "theatrically decorated with Louis XV-style paneling, painted red and gold."

Unlike the rest of the complex with its heavily provenanced furnishings, this museum requires minimal intellectual investment (i.e., fun for kids of all ages). Visitors are greeted by two gilded, ornate circus wagons and a reproduction of an excessively tall clown, likely worn by a fearless individual of average height on stilts. A colossal mural depicting the Ringling Bros/Barnum & Bailey show of the 1970s and 1980s is another made-you-look. Featuring, among many others, aerialist Dolly Jacobs and her father, master clown Lou Jacobs, it also showcases Gunther Gebel-Williams tactfully described by the Ringling website as a "celebrated animal presenter," although PETA and the occasional homesick tiger might disagree.

Along with the glittery and often skimpy outfits worn by both men and women, there are oversized shoes, horns, fake poultry, and other accessories of foolish destruction weaponized by clowns.

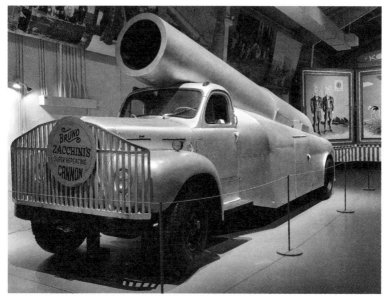

Hopefully, they drew the line at launching human beings from this "clown truck."
SANDRA GURVIS

Many of the exhibits are interactive—walk the wire (safely tethered to the ground); squeeze into a clown car; and have an Instagram moment with the faux tiger, although staff would probably draw the line at climbing into the cannon with the fantasy of being launched across the Big Top.

Additional memorabilia as well as funding for exhibit space also came via a late wealthy benefactor, Howard Tibbals. In fact, an entire wing, the Tibbals Learning Center, is named after him, with the piece de resistance (for some) being a 1920s–1930s replica of the not-coincidentally monikered "Howard Bros. Circus," which is actually a reproduction of the Ringling Bros/Barnum & Bailey Circus during that period. Tibbals began work on his 3,800-square-foot, three-quarter-inch brainchild/obsession in 1956, when he was a freshman engineering student.

Equally eccentric but more subtly presented are the stories and photos of "freak" performers on the museum's second floor, several of whom predated the Ringling Brothers circus. These include Chang and Eng, Siamese twins who were actually from Siam, married two sisters, and settled on a North Carolina plantation in the mid-1800s. In a bizarre, politically incorrect plot twist that out-Kardashians the Kardashians, the now-wealthy brothers not only owned slaves but also had 21 children between them. And then there was General Tom Thumb, aka Charles Stratton, a British person of restricted growth who started performing at age four, married another little person in what arguably had to be the smallest big wedding of the (19th) century, and appeared before Queen Victoria in Buckingham Palace. In contrast were the 6-foot 6-inch, 350-pound Eliza Laurence, aka Madam de Letzi, aka "Swiss Giantess," who at age 51 and penniless, committed suicide by jumping off the Waterloo Bridge in London, and Genevieve, a "black albino" from the Caribbean. Also meeting a tragic end was 2-foot 7-inch Dutch entertainer John Wormberg, who was displayed in a box until—oops—a porter dropped him into a Rotterdam River.

Speaking of trains—wrecks or otherwise—is the circa 1905 *Wisconsin* displayed in all its refurbished glory. Used by John and Mable to commute between their New York and Sarasota homes and mostly by John as he traveled across the country in the quest for circus acts, "at 79 feet long, the car contains sleeping compartments, a kitchen, bathrooms and crew quarters," states the Circus Museum's descriptive plaque. Decorated in "inlaid mahogany, ornate moldings and stained glass," it remains a gleaming testament to post–Victorian era elegance.

John Ringling's butler, a Black man named Emmanuel "Taylor" Gordon, traveled with John and Mable and provided insight into their lives, both at home and en route:

After the New York run we were making ready to go west. [Mrs. Ringling's] dressmaker had just finished her new

Taylor Gordon, far left, shows off a successful catch with his former boss, John Ringling.
THE JOHN AND MABLE RINGLING MUSEUM OF ART ARCHIVES, PAPERS OF JOHN RING-LING, COLLECTION OF RINGLING FAMILY PHOTOGRAPHIC ALBUMS

summer wardrobe. Among the dresses, she had one phantom red all over, shoes to match. . . . He and her [*sic*] was going to the Waldorf Astoria for a late dinner and dance. I was going by the hall to his room when we all three kinda met. He spied . . . her flaming red dress, and made her take it off. I didn't say a thing, but she looked at me. I must have registered the wrong smile, because the next morning she asked me to press the canvas cover that they put over the carpet when they went away for the summer. The canvas is fully twenty feet by forty feet. I told her, yes I'd do it, but the more I thought of it, the more I thought I'd spoiled my job there by knowing too many things. (Taylor Gordon, *Born to Be*, 149)

Shortly after that incident, Gordon left the Ringlings' service and pursued a successful career as a vaudeville performer during the 1920s and 1930s, thanks in part to John Ringling's support.

Educated, Part 1: Tales from Clown College

Although Snopes has yet to verify, more than one source has pointed out that the Ringling Bros/Barnum & Bailey Clown College was harder to get into than Harvard, if only based on the massive proportion of applicants to limited available spaces. But its establishment in Venice in 1968 by then-owner Irvin Feld was no joke. "There was a real need for new talent because many of the clowns were aging out of the circus," observes Peggy Williams, one of the first female graduates (1970) who also had the distinction of being the first female clown offered a Ringling/B & B contract. Its acceptance was part of the deal—if they were even chosen. At 10 weeks and with no tuition, and with the only expenses being room and board, the course was also a whole lot cheaper than the Ivy League, even back then. And although it was intensive, involving long hours of practice, it was more fun as well. Rather than finance, engineering, and nuclear physics, students studied juggling, acrobatics, stilt walking, improvisation, choreography, and makeup.

According to Williams, "some senior clowns saw the college as a threat" because clowning later in life was viewed as an option when performing became too physically difficult. Yet students were taught and mentored by skilled, experienced clowns. "Everyone was very supportive and generous with their knowledge, even though they had to make special dressing and bathroom accommodations since I was the only 'girl.'" A former deaf education major at the University of Wisconsin, she observed that Clown College "taught me how to use small and big movements to communicate nonverbally to large crowds. You are telling a story, but in a different way." She stayed with the circus for decades and now works in the archives at the Ringling Museum.

Clown College also helped figuratively and (possibly literally, while at the circus) launch the careers of Broadway performer Bill Irwin; magician Penn Jillette (Penn and Teller), and playwright and lyricist Murray Horwitz, who today works as a broadcaster and arts administrator in Washington, DC. In 1970, when he

Clown College proved to be a launching point for many successful careers, including that of Murray Horwitz (pictured) and Peggy Williams.
COURTESY OF MURRAY HORWITZ

applied and was accepted, Horwitz had to get permission from Kenyon, the small liberal arts college he attended, to obtain a leave of absence. Horwitz describes himself as a bit of a comedian and goof-off in those days: "I don't think they would have allowed it for anybody else, but for me, they thought it made sense."

Although hardly from a circus family—his father was a surgeon—Horwitz not only received their blessing but was also hired to perform in the circus, where he stayed for three years. Between training and the grueling performance schedule, "I had to work hard for the first time in my life and after about five months of being unfunny was finally advised [by a senior clown] to stop trying so hard and just be myself. Instantly I started to get laughs." Still "while I had figured out about 70 or 80 percent of what makes a good clown, I was unwilling to spend another 20 years to learn the rest. There were other things I wanted to do." Like originating and co-writing the Broadway hit *Ain't Misbehavin'*, for example. Based on the music of Fats Waller, it won Tony, Obie, Emmy, Grammy, and New York Drama Critics' Circle awards.

After graduating some 1,300 clowns, the college closed in 1997. But its spirit lives on at Sarasota's one- to two-week Circus Summer Camp at the Circus Arts Conservatory, which teaches children aspects of noncreepy clowning such as trapeze, juggling, and unicycle riding as well as holding some classes for adults.

Educated, Part Two: The Ringling College of Art + Design, the Ringling Librar(ies), and Ringling Museum Archives

Ringling College of Art + Design

Lack of funds prevented John Ringling from opening his own art school in conjunction with the museum; this proved to be a blessing in the long run. But in 1931, he was hit up for a donation to create an art school at what is now Florida Southern College (FSC) by then-president Dr. Ludd M. Spivey. Ringling, recently widowed, nearly bankrupt and dealing with a raft of health and personal problems including a hasty and problematic second marriage, didn't have the cash but still convinced Spivey to open an FSC-affiliated art school in Sarasota. By 1933, the original School of Fine and Applied Art of the John and Mable Ringling Art Museum had separated from FSC and become an independent nonprofit, shortening its name to what eventually became the much more hip-sounding Ringling College of Art + Design.

This saved the school from the 10 years of neglect that befell Ca' d'Zan and the Museum properties after John died, leaving his assets in shambles and limbo while the State of Florida and John's nephew and executor, John Ringling North, sorted out the mess. Instead, during the 1930s and 1940s, the college stablished itself as a separate but equal entity that focused on fine, rather than circus, arts and attracted cutting-edge and sometimes controversial instructors and students. Among the latter two were costume designer Guy Saunders, who gussied up everyone from evangelist Aimee Semple McPherson to burlesque dancer Sally Rand, and Zelda Fitzgerald, wife of F. Scott Fitzgerald, who according to *The First Fifty Years—Ringling School of Art and Design* "attended . . . along with her nurse, as a part of her therapy in a North Carolina Sanitarium."

A fully accredited, degree-granting institution, today the 48-acre campus enrolls over 1,600 students from all over the world who study everything from the business of art and design to virtual reality development, along with film, graphic design, game art, photography, and more. As with the Clown College, "faculty members are all professional artists, designers, and scholars who actively pursue their own work outside the classroom," according to the Ringling College website. Notable grads include David Bromstad (HGTV personality), Michelle Phan (makeup artist/YouTube star), and Bret Iwan (21st-century voice of Mickey Mouse). But unlike clowns whose old-school weirdness has garnered some bad press, this college continues to expand and grow, filling an educational niche for burgeoning technologies in graphic design, animation, and even fine arts.

Ringling Art Library and Archives and Goldstein Library at the Ringling College

Sarasota has two "Ringling" libraries, which can get a bit confusing. But along with being separate entities, they are about as different as two libraries can be. Located in the Education Center on Museum grounds and only open a few hours daily, the *Ringling Art Library* is "one of the largest and most comprehensive art research libraries in the southeastern United States," notes the Ringling website. Although today it has 70,000+ holdings, its genesis was over 800 art books and auction catalogues acquired by John Ringling as he learned the finer points of acquisition. Originally housed in Ca' d'Zan, the collection "includes some rare versions of classic art history volumes that students still study today." And that's on top of hundreds of databases with auction records and information about contemporary artists as well as manuscripts covering everything from the Renaissance and Baroque periods to circus art to glass sculpture and more.

Also on the museum grounds are the *Ringling Archives*. An appointment is needed to access this trove of handbills, art prints, circus papers, business records, photos, and many other items. But it's mostly for scholars and researchers; few visit the Ringling with the express purpose of checking out newspaper clippings from 1816.

With an open, airy layout and dramatic water views, the modern, geometrically enthusiastic *Alfred R. Goldstein Library at the Ringling College of Art + Design* represents the antithesis of the traditional musty, "keep quiet" libraries. Completed in 2017, with some 49,000 square feet of "a bold, collaborative space that roars with the creativity of students and alumni," according to architect Shepley Bulfinch, it offers a minimum of books and private places to curl up but a maximum of computer access opportunities, collaboration spaces, and borderline garish wall murals.

"Chick's" Second Golden Egg: The Fabulous Asolo Theater

One might wonder how a theater named after a town in Italy whose origin was the 15th-century residence of the Queen of Cyprus ended up in Sarasota, Florida. Repurposed as a theater in 1798, the ornate, rococo U-shaped space was redesigned a mere 50 years later, "leading scholars to conclude that the renovation duplicated the original plan," according to the Ringling website. Dismantled in 1931, its mere existence is an act of serendipity.

The interior and furnishings were purchased by Adolph Loewi, a German Jewish arts and antiquities dealer who fled Italy in 1939. During the ensuing years, while Adolf Hitler trashed Europe, Loewi's stock was relocated to a safe place, thanks to associate Alessandro Morandotti, who returned it to him (Loewi, not Hitler) after the war.

The Ringling purchased it for a mere $8,000 in 1949 thanks to Loewi's friend Chick Austin, who also happened to be its director, although limited finances and the Korean War prevented its construction in a separate building. So the ever-ingenious Austin temporarily installed the seating and stage in the museum's auditorium, where, in early 1952, not only did he organize an opening gala featuring operas from Mozart and Pergolesi but also designed the costumes.

Unfortunately, Austin had passed away when the building currently housing the Asolo was completed six years later. Successor Kenneth Donahue—with the help of the City of Sarasota once they figured out that this could put it on the cultural map—planned an opening celebration that also included opera "in the glittering jewel" that was now called by the Ringling website the Historic Asolo Theater, as well as dancing and costumes in Ca' d'Zan and fireworks on the bay. "It was a party worthy of John and Mable themselves," lavishly covered by *Life* magazine, which was the mid-20th-century equivalent of winning the internet.

Besides, being John Ringling wasn't all it was cracked up to be, especially after June 8, 1929.

Chapter 11

John Ringling's Final Act

Two individuals might be deemed responsible for the unraveling of John Ringling: his beloved wife, Mable, and Sam Gumpertz, circus impresario and freak hunter. Ringling's failing health also contributed to his downfall and the circumstances that led to his death on December 2, 1936.

After wintering in Ca' d'Zan for only three years, Mable passed away at age 54 in New York on June 8, 1929. Like the big cats in the circus (and cats everywhere), she was very good at hiding her symptoms.

> For several years Aunt Mable had been keeping a secret. So well did she counterfeit that no one, except her doctor, certainly not Uncle John, knew that she was mortally ill of a complication of diabetes and Addison's disease. Early in 1929 strength of will could no longer overcome their ravages. That spring she took to her bed, and with her customary consideration for her husband, died very quickly. (Henry Ringling North, *The Circus Kings*, 161–62)

"For twenty-five years [Mable] had provided a domestic stability that . . . constantly shielded [John] from . . . outside business transgressors," noted Aaron De Groft in "John Ringling in *Perpetua Memoria*," adding that the Ringlings did well in choosing each other. "The king of the big top did not seek out a flamboyant or wealthy socialite because he was not so flamboyant himself in his personal life. Mable appears fortunate to have found in John someone who delighted in sharing and cultivating her interests in travel, art and culture."

A private person, Mable loved all things natural and beautiful, including birds with sharp beaks and claws and also, of course, John.
THE JOHN AND MABLE RINGLING MUSEUM OF ART ARCHIVES, PAPERS OF JOHN RING-LING, COLLECTION OF RINGLING FAMILY PHOTOGRAPHIC ALBUMS

By all accounts, her death devastated John Ringling. It also precipitated a stumble that led to many others.

THE HAAG BUCKS

While there's no questioning John's love for Mable, the old adage "women mourn, men replace" also applies. By 1930, even though John, like the rest of the country, was reeling from the stock market crash of October 28 of the previous year, within months he was out and about again, traveling internationally and dining with friends. On the Fourth of July, while in Amsterdam, he met New Yorker Emily Haag Buck: "She was thirty-four by her own account, or forty-five according to Ringling's estimate; he was then sixty-three," notes Weeks in *Ringling: The Florida Years* (264). "[She] was an attractive socialite—exceedingly chic, tall, and blonde. They were both sophisticated, worldly-wise people—he after twenty-five years of domestic accord, she after one brief failure." Yet perhaps because of their hasty union—they married the following December in the office of Jersey City Mayor Frank "Boss" Hague—"neither developed an understanding of the other's nature or character."

"The comely Emily, who enjoyed throwing cocktail parties at home and the night life among the swells in clubs from New York to Miami and Palm Beach, was undoubtedly impressed with the trappings of the circus king's wealth," observed the Ringling site. "For his part, Ringling was probably taken by Emily's sophisticated looks, intelligence, sparkling personality—and she also had plenty of cash on hand, an enviable commodity as the Depression wore on."

Had she been paying closer attention, Emily might have been clued into the coming storm when John asked to borrow $50,000 shortly before they wed. He also "proffered her a document to sign renouncing her dower rights," continued the site. The purpose of this was to protect the art collection and museum because under Florida law, the widow is entitled to one third of her husband's estate in the absence of a will (dower rights). "He said she signed on the dotted line and tore it up later; she said she tore it up but had never signed it," setting the "he said, she said" stage for a rocky marriage and headline-grabbing divorce. Part of what was at stake was the preservation of John's art collection, which he later claimed that Mable, rather than himself, had purchased.

And while this strategy seemed effective and nearly all of his art holdings remained at the museum, Rembrandt's *The Evangelist* was indeed sold in 1939 to meet a debt when Emily foreclosed on a loan against five of John's other paintings. The remainder was paid off in cash installments.

Still, the beginning was promising, with a gala winter season in Sarasota that included a reception held by brother Charles's widow, Edith. "The paper called it the most brilliant party of the season, complete with an orchestra that played into the night and attended by the Who's Who of local society," continued the Ringling site.

STANDING TALL ON A DWINDLING WALLET

But there was an elephant in the room and it wasn't from the circus. By early 1931, although Sarasota County was so strapped for cash it was unable to pay its teachers and temporarily closed its schools, "country club members were offered such diversions as a Depression dance with the theme 'How to have fun though broke,'" observed Weeks. Among those dressed for indigency was Emily Ringling, member of the planning committee, who "appeared in a native Cuban costume and a necklace of new potatoes." Lucky for her, there was no Instagram, as she likely would have been canceled more quickly than she'd wed.

But within months, Emily would tire of small spud Sarasota, preferring the larger arena of the Big Apple, although, since John's apartment rent was overdue and in order to avoid eviction, they were forced to rough it at the Ritz-Carlton when they visited. "Her life style of having friends in for cocktails and the disruption of his preferred quiet solitude rankled [John], and, too, her sister and nephew lived at Ca' d'Zan, Ringling's peaceful retreat," added the Ringling site. She also spent money freely on parties, clothes, and jewelry.

Fiddling while Rome burns: John and Emily Ringling (right) at the Sara de Soto celebration in 1931. Party down!
THE JOHN AND MABLE RINGLING MUSEUM OF ART ARCHIVES, PAPERS OF JOHN RING-LING, COLLECTION OF RINGLING FAMILY PHOTOGRAPHIC ALBUMS

And like many couples where one partner is fiscally sound while the other struggles with debt, they fought about finances. John's troubles began well before Emily came into the picture. In the spring of 1929, he failed to show up for the annual signing of the circus contract at Madison Square Garden (MSG), where some version of the Ringling/Barnum & Bailey shows had played for over half a century. No big deal for someone who "was quite accustomed to making engagements with important people and breaking them cavalierly," remarked Ringling North.

But it was for MSG, creating an opportunity that new management was waiting for, to not only increase the rent but also replace the circus's regular Friday night performance with highly lucrative but sometimes dodgy prize fights. None of these, especially the latter, sat well with Ringling, who prided himself on a family-friendly, essentially straightforward operation. The end result, according to Ringling North, was "a violent scene [in which] Uncle John told them with anatomical exactitude precisely where they could put their contract and announced that the circus would open at the 22nd Regiment Armory."

Along with getting mad, Ringling got even, sort of, borrowing $2 million to purchase his biggest rival, the American Circus Corporation, which did agree to the MSG contract. And while American Circus was a solid concern, the expense of which John believed he could offset by selling stocks to the public, Black Monday happened, and soon most people couldn't even afford groceries. The result was a financial albatross that encumbered him for the rest of his days.

The acquisition also helped set the stage for the treachery that cost John the management of his own circus. Although John made the American Circus purchase independently, as money grew tighter, he "succeeded in transferring . . . [its] ownership to Ringling Brothers, despite the justified reluctance" of his other two partners, explained Ringling North. That would be Charles's widow, Edith, and Alfred's son, Richard, who died in 1931, leaving his third to his wife, Aubrey. Unlike his brothers, with whom he was on an even footing and who reined him in, at least with regard to circus matters, it was typical of John to make decisions without consulting Edith, who after a period of mourning, was once again involved with circus and civic issues and had formed her own alliances. The main involvement of Richard, a Montana rancher, was to sign the back of the annual $1 million dividend check.

John Ringling's real estate and railroad investments were also bleeding money. Additionally, the Feds were circling over the carcass of his affairs, looking for back taxes and remittance of fines for regulatory noncompliance to the eventual tune of some $13 million. By 1931, he had over a hundred lawsuits pending for, among many other things, violating antitrust laws.

Such stress would be debilitating for even a young, healthy person. Although John Ringling had weathered storms before by glossing over troubles and forging ahead where no showman had gone before, this time the elephant had become an unstoppable, thundering herd.

A CONGRESS OF FREAKS: SNEAKER OF THE HOUSE

John Ringling and Sam Gumpertz had been friends for over 40 years. So in the spring of 1932, when John suffered a life-threatening blood clot in his leg and needed a hideaway where he could recuperate in peace, he fled to the Half Moon Hotel in Coney Island, owned by his "brother from another mother" and one of the few nonrelatives he actually trusted.

Both men loved and spent a lifetime in the circus and amusement business and both were self-made, although Gumpertz lacked the strong familial ties of the Ringling brotherhood. They were also around the same age—John was born in 1866 and Gumpertz about two years later. Like Ringling, who had introduced him to Sarasota along with other cronies, Gumpertz was a strong community booster, persuading the New York Giants to come to the area for spring training, donating land and funds for a hospital and summer camp for socially disadvantaged children, and working with Ringling and Owen Burns on the development of Lido Key and other local projects. "Sam Gumpertz had the showman's outgoing nature, and his easy, friendly manner made him popular in the Sarasota community," observed Weeks. Unlike John Ringling, who, depending on the mood of the moment, was either lionized or villainized by the local press.

Gumpertz's backstory is cinematic. He literally ran away to join the circus at age nine, working as an acrobat until landing on his head after a fall from a human pyramid. He recovered, wisely avoiding that activity for the remainder of his life. He became a cowboy, eventually joining the Buffalo Bill show and performing

John Ringling at the 1928 Sara Sota pageant festivities with, left to right, Frances Booth, J. W. Burns, Mrs. A. E. Cummer, Frances Edwards (daughter of A. B. Edwards, first mayor of Sarasota), and none other than the Machiavellian Sam Gumpertz.

with the Rough Riders. Among his many accomplishments are the discovery and management of magician Harry Houdini, the builder and manager of Coney Island's Dreamland amusement park, and the creator and promoter of Brooklyn's Brighton Beach. He and John Ringling often traveled together, where he acted as John's spokesperson and/or worked with him on collaborative enterprises.

However, unlike the mostly G-rated Ringlings, Gumpertz had a taste for the truly bizarre. He was single-handedly responsible for what became known as the Congress of Freaks, a mid-1920s agglomeration of human oddities associated with Ringling Bros/Barnum & Bailey and other venues. Today, that sideshow can be found in Washington, DC.

Legislate this: The 1924 Congress of Freaks is now in session!
TIBBALS CIRCUS COLLECTION OF PHOTOGRAPHS, PHOTOGRAPHER EDWARD J. KELTY
(AMERICAN, 1888–1967), 1924

According to *Reader's Digest*, Gumpertz "almost cornered the floating supply of giants, midgets, fat women, three-legged men, Bushman, plate-lipped Ubangis, albino [Africans], giraffe-necked ladies and blue-scarred Somalis. . . . He has had the cream of the bearded ladies, dog-faced boys, missing links, steeple-headed and cylinder-headed folks, grown-together show people, India-rubber men," a total of some 3,800 "what-is-its." For nearly 25 years "he had his heart set on importing a tribe of pygmies from Africa," although "all the pygmy chiefs who have been approached thus far insist that their constituents would not like America." How rude.

Although Gumpertz had an altruistic streak and provided an opportunity for folks who might not otherwise be able to make a living wage, he could be ruthless when it came to business dealings. And had John Ringling been 100 percent, he might have noticed the warning signs. Since John was isolated from his usual contacts in Sarasota and New York, Gumpertz was able to control the narrative "to conceal the plans of his creditors and isolate [John] from competent legal help," stated Weeks.

A CONFEDERACY OF JUDASES

But someone did have his best interests at heart, if only John been willing to listen. According to local historian Jeff LaHurd, John described his marriage to Emily as "just continuous nagging and scolding, finding fault with everything, cursing, screaming, quarreling. . . . She always used the word son-of-a-bitch and committed acts of extreme cruelty and habitual indulgence in . . . ungovernable temper."

Yet "despite their sometimes violent disagreements, Emily tried to protect him from some of the worst invasions of his assets," observed Weeks. But as was typical of men of that era, John believed that women had little knowledge of and therefore should not be involved with business affairs. Although by this time, his two equal partners in the circus, Edith and Aubrey, were of the "fairer sex" persuasion and especially Edith resented John's history of roughshod treatment. Yet Emily, who tried to get him a lawyer to protect his investments in the circus and other assets was dismissed, according to Weeks, as "stealing his papers."

A July 1932 meeting with Edith, Aubrey, and his creditors blew John Ringling's world apart. John believed that they were there to help, including the creditors, Allied Owners and New York Investors, since Gumpertz had persuaded them to purchase the circus promissory note from its original holder, the Prudence Company.

> When [John] limped into that luxurious office he was utterly dumbfounded and confused to find who were his enemies. He looked dumbly from Edith to Aubrey, his close Wall Street friend William Greve, who represented Allied Owners, and to Sam Gumpertz. Though he may have been autocratic and foolish in his dealings with Aunt Edith, he believed he had guarded her interests. To Aubrey he had shown great kindness. To find them arrayed against him was a fearful shock because of

his strong feeling of family solidarity. He was almost as shaken by the implacable attitude of Gumpertz, who up to that moment had been so solicitous for his health, so warm in his professions of friendship. (Ringling North, *The Circus Kings*, 166)

What transpired could be likened to a Greek tragedy. Delivered by what Ringling North called a "carefully thought-out ultimatum" by none other than Gumpertz, was a threat to throw the circus into bankruptcy and to take John's beloved art collection should he not cede to their demands for control. Even the circus's attorney John M. Kelley was advising the opposition: "Had Uncle John had a good lawyer of his own, he would have been advised that it was legally impossible to throw the circus into bankruptcy without a long-drawn-out lawsuit," continued Ringling North. "As it was, John Ringling did not know where to turn."

So he caved, choosing personal ruin over the shutdown of the circus. "Sam Gumpertz was to be general manager in complete charge of running the circus—he had no experience in circus management," stated Ringling North. "Edith and Aubrey Ringling and [lawyer] John M. Kelly [*sic*] were to be vice-presidents."

And no one, including the public, was none the wiser, especially since the press had mostly focused on John's illness, assuming that to be the reason for his stepping aside. Even his friends and business acquaintances had no idea what was really going on.

John struggled to remain involved in the circus, including trying to negotiate a contract with the world-famous Christiani equestrian act. Then, in December 1932 he suffered a debilitating stroke. "He managed to stagger part way to the door in an attempt to get home, and collapsed," recalled Ringling North. "Crumpled in the pocket of [his] suit was . . . a telegram informing him that he must cease his negotiations with the Christianis and, furthermore, if in the future he tried to take any part in the operation of

Although he had to use a cane and at certain times, a wheelchair, John Ringling remained resilient, fighting the forces gathered against him.
THE JOHN AND MABLE RINGLING MUSEUM OF ART ARCHIVES, PAPERS OF JOHN RING-LING, COLLECTION OF RINGLING FAMILY PHOTOGRAPHIC ALBUMS

the circus, 'we will hold a stockholders' meeting and turn you out.' It was signed 'Sam Gumpertz.'"

Gumpertz also went on to foreclose on Sarasota's El Vernona Hotel owned by his other Sarasota bro, Owen Burns. What a guy!

THE LAST PARADE

Thus marked the beginning of the final act for John Ringling, the last survivor of the original Ringling Brothers. And unlike the usual grand circus finale, there was no feel-good ending nor even the sense of closure and peace that can come with the passing of someone who has made a major impact on human affairs.

The divorce from Emily continued to drive splinters into John's already failing health. Although the stroke had left him partially paralyzed, Emily continued to entertain guests in their Park Avenue apartment—apparently they had caught up with back rent—although it sent "[John's] blood pressure and pulse rate soaring," stated Weeks. Emily reluctantly went back to Sarasota with John in the spring of 1933, where he suffered another stroke that affected his speech and movement, adding fuel to an already volatile situation. "Emily's once rich and vigorous husband had changed into a fretting invalid," continued Weeks. Unpaid bills piled up, servants went without wages, and there were daily quarrels that could have easily been avoided had Emily decided to stay in her corner of the huge mansion they both enjoyed.

So John filed for divorce, although apparently Emily had no idea.

> By a mischance, Emily was served with a summons not at home, as he intended, but in a shop on Main Street. Confronted with that unexpected blow in a public place, she became visibly ill. Even in the comparative freedom of life-styles in the early 1930s, there remained a social stigma for women whose husbands divorced them. (Weeks, *Ringling: The Florida Years*, 281)

So began a Depression-era version of Amber Heard vs. Johnny Depp. Although they reconciled briefly—according to John, Emily had gotten on her knees and begged him to stay—by the end of 1933, John moved back to Ca' d'Zan permanently—alone—while

Emily remained in New York. Several months later, in March 1934, he filed for divorce again with the claim of "extreme cruelty," this time retaining a couple of lawyers. When the divorce became final in July 1936, it was reportedly the most expensive in the history of Florida to date.

Of course, Emily had her own version of events, not surprisingly the polar opposite of John's. Mostly they revolved around collecting money and her dower rights. She fought the terms of the divorce, even after John's passing.

The legal actions drained Emily's accounts. According to Gene Plowden in *Those Amazing Ringlings and Their Circus*, "soon after John received his final decree, one of [his] attorneys . . . died and his partner married [Emily]." The Ringling site stated that she was engaged in 1948 "to the wealthy Harold Kittinger." Although he supposedly intended to give his "beloved fiancé" one half of his $5 million estate, Kittinger died unexpectedly during a trip and— surprise!—the will that surfaced instead bequeathed 1,000 shares of his company to "my dear friend." When John passed away in December 1936, he left Emily $1. Poor Emily—she worked hard for the money, but she didn't get treated right.

Despite the swirling brouhaha, the remainder of John Ringling's days were at least on the surface, comparatively tame. Although he recovered part of his physical faculties, "his power of instantaneous, imperious decision was gone," noted Ringling North. During the last couple of years, along with sometimes being confined to a wheelchair, he became frightened and mistrustful of even his closest family members and associates, including John and Henry Ringling North, who remained by his side, even though he eventually disinherited them and greatly reduced a planned stipend to their mother and his sister, Ida, to only $5,000 a year. This made him unable to recognize various solutions that might have forgone his dying with only $311 in the bank, although his estate was appraised at some $23.5 million.

Still, John was able to remain in Ca' d'Zan, thanks to the constant companionship of his loyal nurse Ina Sanders. John's sister, Ida, and her sons, Henry and John Ringling North, also assisted him. John Ringling North, who resuscitated and updated the circus in the 1940s and 1950s after he took it over in 1937 also helped navigate the inevitable financial crises that arose as creditors, lawyers, and Uncle Sam attempted to collect debts and seize assets. Henry Ringling North described his own duties as a "business agent, chauffeur, handyman, and sometimes cook."

Lack of funds also made it extremely difficult to maintain Ca' d'Zan and the museum. Dampness, the salty sea climate, and other types of benign neglect took their toll; not much was done to offset the inevitable damage. This would come back to bite both attractions in the coming years as the State of Florida and then Florida State University struggled with various solutions.

But there was still circus in the old Ringling yet. Shortly before his death, recalls Henry Ringling North, John proposed a road trip to check out the Cole Brothers circus in Pensacola. While they waited for the parade to begin,

> [John] sat absolutely silent staring down at the gathering crowd—the small boys running about and roughhousing, parents and just people buying pennants and whips and those familiar whirly birds from the vendors, little girls in frilly dresses staring big-eyed up the cleared roadway, and the inevitable mongrel pups dashing madly back and forth. . . . The thump of a drum and a wind-borne blast of music brought a complete hush. Just like the kids, I was straining my eyes up the street. I saw the eight horses with nodding plumes of the band wagon round the corner.
>
> Then the full blast of sound hit us, the gay, raucous blare of brass playing circus music. It got louder and louder and behind the tootling musicians I could see

red-and-gold howdahs rolling and pitching on the stately gray backs of the elephants. . . . Then I thought to look at Uncle John. He was sitting absolutely motionless in his chair and tears were streaming like miniature cascades from his eyes.

I saw with him the Ringling band led by white-whiskered Yankee Robinson come down Broadway in Baraboo—Al and Alf T., Charles blowing mightily on his trombone, and Otto lambasting the big bass drum. And capering along with a French horn wound around his shoulder, a gangling young musician-clown. . . . I saw the heavy work teams and the farmer boys guiding our spring wagons with their pathetic homemade decorations. . . . Then, in an Einsteinian relativity of time, the procession lengthened. There went the ferocious, man-eating hyena, the dusty brown bear, and the glowering bald eagle; elk, lions, monkeys, a deer; Aunt Louise wrapped in a boa constrictor; and, very proudly, Babylon and Fannie, those first ponderous pachyderms.

Time stopped. The real calliope was passing out of sight followed by a swarming mass of children young and old. Uncle John pushed himself out of his chair with enormous difficulty and clung to my shoulder. "Time to go home, Buddy," he said. (Ringling North, *The Circus Kings*, 175–77)

By early 1936, Ringling's physical health seemed to be actually improving, and there were some signs that his financial affairs might also turn around. But at the beginning of November, the federal court in Tampa ordered the forced sale of Ca' d'Zan. "Its impending loss turned out to be a final blow," observed Weeks. Shortly thereafter, while in his Park Avenue home in New York City, John Ringling became ill with pneumonia.

His great gold bed was surrounded: the North family, his servants, Nurse Sanders, his physician, and one friend, Frank Hennessy. In his last moments, he called repeatedly for his sister, Ida. Age seventy was old for a Ringling. In a career of more than fifty years he had met the world's standards for success. He had accumulated a fortune, controlled a monopoly, and lived in a palace. (Weeks, *Ringling: The Florida Years*, 295)

On December 2, at age 70, John Ringling passed away. Although it marked the end of the era, it created the unique cultural oasis that is Sarasota today.

Chapter 12

The Modern Circus That Is Sarasota

The period following John's Ringling's death was like his life, full of drama, excitement, and unpredictable twists and turns. Along with circus performers and managers, personal friends, and business associates, his New York funeral was attended by family members, including Ida and her children, John, Henry, and Salome, as well as descendants of the original brothers—except for the Charles Ringling family, who remained notably absent. That rat, Sam Gumpertz, also stayed away.

Almost immediately, the fallout began, or as Henry D. Frost, attorney for the executors understated, "financial entanglements of unprecedented complexity," the attempted resolution of which primarily took place in the county court of Sarasota. In one corner was the State of Florida, recipients of the art museum and Ca' d'Zan. In the other were the trustees John and Henry Ringling North and Randolph Wadsworth, Salome's husband, responsible for the dissemination of the assets owed to some 71 creditors, according to Weeks in *Ringling: The Florida Years*. These ranged from $3.25 (the *Sarasota Herald-Tribune*) to over $13 million (the IRS) and all manner of sums in between.

Such wranglings—as well as the fate of the family circus after John Ringling's death—could in themselves fill and have been subjects of other books, including Weeks's. Ca' d'Zan and the museum and were also impacted, as mentioned in chapters 8 and 9. As discussed in chapter 11, Emily spent much of her savings trying to claim her dower rights, making her an easy target for negative publicity. But perhaps the most adversely affected were John's support staff—Bertha Verby, the Ca' d'Zan housekeeper, and John's nurse, Ina Sanders, who received no payment for her last three years of service—not to mention various merchants and trades-people who repaired and maintained the home and museum. They needed their wages to pay the bills; according to Weeks, Verby didn't even have the funds for food for herself or her dog.

MORE "WHERE'S WALDO?" THAN "WHO IS BURIED IN RINGLING'S GRAVE?"

"When Ringling died, flags flew at half-mast across the city and his body laid in state at the art museum," stated one research-er's account. Well, not exactly. According to the *New York Times*, the half-mast flags were at the circus's Sarasota Winter Quarters and the relocation of John—in death, reunited with his beloved Mable—would take place at the museum, although the words "lie in state" were also involved, sowing the seeds for the mental image of visitors lining up to view John and Mable in situ in the middle of the Astor Crème Salon.

Although they had to cut costs elsewhere, when it came to completing their plans for the museum, one thing John and Mable didn't budge on was the fact that they wanted to be buried on museum grounds. (Of course, by the time things were finalized, they couldn't budge anyway, but that's beside the point.) Rather than in the middle of the museum, their desired resting place was under the bridge connecting two wings, near the statue of David, in what Weeks described as "a mosaic lined chamber partly hid-den behind an elaborate perforated alabaster screen [with] two sarcophagi mounted with sculptured reclining figures." Talk about fancy! Visitors could check out the carved effigies of J and M resting (hopefully) in peace in their ornate crypt, with its vaulted marbled ceiling and mortuary-style floor.

Creepy by today's standards—on-site graves are usually rele-gated to but still somewhat unnervingly found in U.S. presidential libraries, overseas churches, and Old World art galleries—John may have also been thinking about extending brotherly rivalry into the Great Beyond. "Charles Ringling's strikingly beautiful pink marble mausoleum is easily visible from the road off of U.S. 301 in Oneco at the Manasota Memorial Park," noted historian Jeff LaHurd in the *Sarasota Herald-Tribune*.

Things didn't quite work out as planned. Mable's sudden passing and John's quick remarriage also made it "a somewhat awkward issue; yet after his separation and divorce, Ringling never revived the idea," stated Weeks. Instead, he re-thought the concept of turning his final resting place into a sideshow and opted to be buried outside the museum on the grounds, "although he never finalized this decision either." The original crypt is now used for storage.

The various court claims dragged on, as did the final decision regarding their interment. Even in death, the couple still traveled quite a bit, by 1958 having been laid to almost-rest in three different places on the East Coast, the longest being 18 years in a New Jersey vault. Eventually, in 1987, after much legal wrangling, museum trustee Henry Ringling North had them relocated to Restlawn Memorial Gardens in Port Charlotte, Florida. Henry's brother John Ringling North had passed away two years earlier, leaving Henry as the primary decision maker regarding such family matters. Despite the fact that John disinherited him and his brother and deeply discounted Ida's stipend shortly before he died, Henry "then decided that he wanted his mother, Ida, buried with [John and Mable], on museum property," explained historian Jeff LaHurd. Ida, who herself had passed in 1950, was nearby, "temporarily" parked in a funeral home in Sarasota.

> Some members of the family disagreed; Ida, they felt, should be buried next to her husband in Baraboo, Wisconsin. A court battle ensued which Henry won, and in a plot of land described by architect Matt Mathes as "modest but fitting," the trio at long last were laid to rest. (LaHurd, *Sarasota Herald-Tribune* website)

That was in June 1991, according to the *Tampa Bay Times*, a very "small, private" un-Ringling-like ceremony tucked away in Mable's Secret Garden. Around 2017 or so, former Ca' d'Zan curator Ron McCarty installed a seven-foot white marble sculpture of Flora, the goddess of flowering plants. Although it was to symbolize Mable's love of gardening, the statue is front and center behind the middle grave, which also happens to be John's. Coincidence? Although John was no longer around to give his opinion, he'd probably think not.

THE CIRCUS IN SARASOTA, PART ONE: THE CIRCUS

Although certain elements of the circus, including juggling, acrobatics, balancing acts, and the now heavily questioned use of animals (see sidebar) have been traced to ancient Rome, the modern-day circus has its roots in England during the 1770s "when Philip Astley, a cavalryman and veteran of the Seven Years War, brought circus elements—acrobatics, riding, and clowning—together in a ring at his riding school near Westminster Bridge in London," stated author and professor Janet M. Davis in the *Smithsonian* magazine.

Trained by one of Astley's students, a Scotsman named John Bill Ricketts introduced the circus to America:

> In April of 1793, some 800 spectators crowded inside a walled, open-air, wooden ring in Philadelphia to watch the nation's first circus performance. Ricketts, a trick rider, and his multicultural troupe of a clown, an acrobat, a rope-walker, and a boy equestrian, dazzled President George Washington and other audience members with athletic feats and verbal jousting. (Davis, *Smithsonian* magazine)

Subsequent fine-tuning and dominance by Joshua Purdy Brown (circa 1802–1834) of Delaware, who first used a tent; Dan

Castello (circa 1832–1909) of Wisconsin; and William Cameron Coup (1837–1895) of Indiana whose Great Circus & Egyptian Caravan provided the template for the present-day circus and suckered in the involvement of impresario P. T. Barnum; and others, both famous and lesser-known, have proven the circus's durability through the ages. It continues to be reimagined, and thanks to John and Charles Ringling, who first came to Sarasota in the early 20th century, Southwest Florida remains an incubator and breeding ground for all things circus. Several circuses are located in and around Sarasota.

Circus Arts Conservatory and Camp
Established in 1949, this large, multitentacled organization offers several programs to the public. These include the *Sailor Circus*, "The Greatest 'Little' Show on Earth," the nation's longest-running youth circus and a top-rated training ground for budding entertainers. Billed as having "circus as it's meant to be seen—award-winning international artists in one ring, under the big top," *Circus Sarasota* has also been around for over 25 years, drawing quite a crowd during its various runs at Benderson Park. More offshoots include *Cirque des Voix*, or "Circus of the Voices," an "exciting collaboration with . . . the spectacle of circus, the power of a megachoir and the thunder of the symphony," according to the website, and even a *Summer Circus Spectacular* at the Ringling complex itself.

Children and adults can also get into the act by taking recreational classes. There's even a circus camp for kids, with a performance at the end. Additionally, "edutainment" outreach is available at schools and health care facilities.

Cirque Italia
Headquartered in Sarasota, this European-style offering has replaced animal acts with water, water everywhere, some 35,000 gallons utilized by performers on a stage that travels from city to city. "Inspired by the element of water, the acts express versatility

Circus, 0; Critters, a Golden Parachute?

John Ringling was ahead of his time when it came to humane(ish) treatment of animals. According to his December 2 obituary in *The New York Times*, "in 1925 [the circus] dropped all animal acts with the explanation that the public had a distaste for the spectacle of a man risking his head by putting it into a lion's mouth" (never mind about the lion's feelings). Some children were reportedly also traumatized by "seeing [performer] Mable Stark in a cage with fourteen snarling tigers and a black jaguar." However, the Ringling/Barnum & Bailey policy of only having "interesting and playful animals such as seals, dogs, horses, elephants" to counteract "the impression . . . that wild animals are taught their tricks by cruel methods" was reneged a few years later when they hired performer Clyde Beatty, who according to the article, "mixed thirty-six lions and ten tigers in a cage when there were more animals in less space" than had ever been done before. Beatty also used a pole to prod recalcitrant critters and shot blanks in their faces when they charged at him. And although he went on to have a successful career in movies and radio, karma kicked in when he was severely bitten by a lion.

Although they had retired their elephants a year earlier to the White Oak Conservation center in Yulee, Florida, after a 146-year run, the Ringling Brothers and Barnum & Bailey Circus ceased production in 2017. As of this writing, Feld plans to relaunch what they likely considered an outdated brand in September 2023. This newest iteration will only feature two-legged performers, launched by the folks that brought the world Monster Jam, Sesame Street Live, and Disney on Ice. Or in Feld hype-speak, "The American icon emerges as a dynamic, multi-platform entertainment franchise. . . . We are innovating all aspects of the live show . . . to create an engaging property that will last another 150 years." Translation: Watch for toys, t-shirts, and theme parks, not to mention a social media presence buoyed by "a documentary that will take the audience backstage to meet the cast and crew and learn what it takes to be part of The Greatest Show On Earth."

People for the Ethical Treatment of Animals (PETA) agrees. "Ringling is returning with a bang, transforming the saddest show

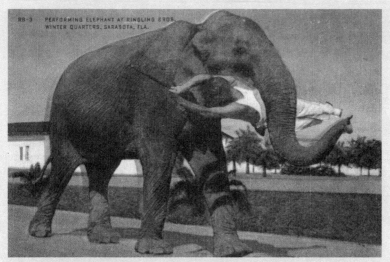

Elephants are no longer a common sight at the circus due to living conditions during their "off" hours.

on Earth into a dazzling display of human ingenuity after 146 years of animal abuse," enthused Rachel Mathews, PETA's foundation director of captive animal law enforcement to CBS News.

Although most other circuses no longer utilize animal acts, there are still a few holdouts: Loomis Bros Circus, Jordan World, Carden International, Royal Hanneford, and Carson & Barnes according to the World Animal Protection Foundation. "Major cities banned the use of bullhooks, whips, or the use of wild animals for entertainment," continues the foundation's blog, which goes on to detail the potential abuse that wild animals on the road can suffer, including spending most of their lives in chains or cages, traveling in boxcars with no climate control, environments that can result in infections, arthritis, and even tuberculosis.

So many circus critters can now join the legions of grateful housecats who are, in general veterinary practice and in some places by law, no longer allowed to be declawed and other caged, domestic pets legally prohibited in many states and localities from being sold at commercial pet stores.

and fluidity through human movement while curtains of rain and fountain jets crisscross in time to each move," states the website. "Laser lights and bubbles also add to the interdimensional effect. . . . [M]ermaids rise from the depths, and even dinosaurs make an appearance. Guests will be surprised, for it's a show of its own!" They might also want to bring rain gear.

Royal Hanneford Circus
Also located in Sarasota, this more traditional circus is one of the few that does feature animals—everything from house cats to tigers to elephants to camels to zebras, bears, and more. They've been around for quite a while; according to their website, tracing their origins to 1690 "with Irish-born Michael Hanneford who toured the dusty roads of rural England with Wombwell's Menagerie, the first show of it's [sic] kind in the British Isles." Descendants, Adrian Poema and Nellie Hanneford Poema and their four children carry on the tradition.

Zerbini Family Circus
Located in nearby Myakka City and Sarasota, yet another family owned/operated circus has been around for over a century. Cast in the imprint of Ringling and not to be confused with the Webb City, Missouri–based Tarzan Zerbini Circus, this Zerbini mostly tours the southern part of the United States.

Others and Circus-Adjacent
Others are a bit farther away, such as the Citrus Circus of Southwest Florida, which provides à la carte "acts" for special events as well as classes and workshops. Related offerings include Aerial Dragon Studios of Tampa, which teaches the aerial arts, and the Dance and Circus Arts of Tampa Bay, to mention a few.

The region is also a font of circus history tours and circus-adjacent attractions. Today, a portion of "JomaR," the railroad car used by John and Mable, lives on as part of Bob's Train, a Sarasota restaurant/museum. Chow down on grilled brie and berries, kielbasa with onions and peppers, burgers, and other fare in one of four historic Ringling cars while enjoying total immersion in circus memorabilia and lore. Led by a former Ringling/Barnum & Bailey marketing executive, Circus Secrets of Sarasota from Discover Sarasota Tours explores circus myths and mysteries and historic neighborhoods via "Dolly the Trolley." Venice Train Depot and Circus Car Museum tours from the Venice Area Historical Society offer further insight into that funky beach town's contribution to its Ringling heritage. Although the depot itself was renovated and converted into a museum at the beginning of the 21st century, the Ringling train car is a new acquisition, featuring re-created living quarters of former performers, videos, and memorabilia.

The region houses numerous circus associations, the most visible of which is the Gibtown Showmen's Club affiliated with International Independent Showmen's Museum in nearby

Inside Bob's Train: It's a circus museum! It's a restaurant!
SANDRA GURVIS

The rides at the Showmen's Museum can only jolt memories, which may be a good thing for some folks.
SANDRA GURVIS

Gibsonton, which was discussed in chapter 10. Although the annual trade show—"the largest array of products pertaining to the amusement industry from around the world"—may only be of interest to amusement business professionals, the museum is worth stopping by. Its display of rides, ornate costumes, and re-creations of various bizarre sideshows is almost guaranteed to bring back childhood memories, especially for the current reigning generation of seniors.

Show Folks of Sarasota is a freestanding members-only social club open to everyone from performers to fans. It might even tempt Groucho Marx, because in order to find out what really goes on there, you have to join. The Circus Ring of Fame honors performers and those behind the scenes, past and present, who have done their bit to keep the circus alive. There are others as well.

THE SARASOTA CIRCUS, PART TWO: THE CITY

Thanks in part to their names emblazoned on streets, buildings, bridges, and of course the museum and home, the Ringling impact on Sarasota remains visible. However, the indirect effects are ongoing and may seem tangential to visitors and even some permanent residents.

Such impacts manifest themselves in many ways and of course are also affected by many of the "founding parents" and subsequent influencers discussed throughout this book. The following are a few of the most apparent.

Sarasota Art Museum (SAM)

A mash-up of a former high school, furniture showroom, and office space at what is now the Ringling College campus, the SAM opened in December 2019, with its claim to fame being a "kunsthalle," meaning a museum without a permanent collection, a traveling art circus. With its main focus on post–World War II and contemporary art, the eclectic, rotating exhibits are showcased in a "white box" gallery and/or soaring cathedral-like tower gallery. Also on tap: educational and performance spaces, gift and coffee shop, and (of course) library/archives.

Marie Selby Botanical Gardens

The "Selby," as it is called, was established in 1973 when Marie Selby bequeathed some 15 acres of her former residence to the foundation formed by her and her husband, William. In the 1920s, the Selbys ran in the same circles as the Ringlings; Marie was a founding member of the Garden Club, and they were also active in the Sarasota Yacht Club. Among other tropical flora and fauna, the downtown campus is "the only botanical garden in the world dedicated to the display and study of epiphytic orchids, bromeliads, gesneriads and ferns," according to the garden's website. In 2020, Bertha Palmer got into the act (kind of) when the Selby acquired 30 acres of her winter estate in Historic Spanish Point in Osprey. "As one of the largest preserves showcasing native Florida plants," it also boasts "an archaeological record that encompasses approximately 5,000 years of Florida prehistory."

Van Wezel Performing Arts Hall
Built in 1968–1969 with Sarasota bond monies and a bequest from its namesake philanthropists and in an exquisite setting next to Sarasota Bay, the Van Wezel has the dubious honor of being "the world's only purple seashell-shaped theater," according to a Norton Center for the Arts history. This totally makes sense given it was the 1960s and, after all, Sarasota and the circus. Not surprisingly, this has lent itself to some controversy, especially given the lack of center aisles, creating a potential fire and pit stop hazard. The Van Wezel's days may be numbered since it will soon be called Sarasota Performing Arts Foundation, with a new performing arts center being constructed in the recently spruced up Bay Park.

THE SARASOTA ARTS SCENE
Partially due to the quirkiness inherent in the circus and the respectability lent to it by the Ringling family, the Sarasota arts scene has its own unique flavor and viability, remaining vibrant and accessible as people of all ages are drawn to and support it, whether as entertainers, support staff/volunteers, regular patrons, or occasional ticket purchasers. Along with a professional opera, ballet, and orchestra, live theater offerings run the full gamut, ranging from the more homegrown Florida Studio Theatre and the Westcoast Black Theatre Group to the Asolo Repertory Theater (Asolo Rep), the largest Equity theater in the Southeastern United States. Nearby, the Venice Theatre prides itself as being one the most active community theaters in the United States while the Manatee Performing Arts Center grew from a small troupe of part-time locals in the 1940s to a year-round, fully staffed enterprise with a wide range of musical and dramatic offerings.

In fact, Sarasota is rife with artistic endeavors of all stripes, from the Marietta Museum of Whimsy, which takes itself fairly seriously in "collecting, preserving and exhibiting works of Artistic and Whimsical importance," to the Hermitage Artist Retreat on Manasota Key, such a dream gig that rather than apply on their own, playwrights, visual artists, composers, authors, and others must be nominated to be selected. And just about everything else in between too numerous to mention here.

A NOT-SO-TROUBLED PARADISE

The region itself is experiencing growing pains, from the real estate boom, which escalates housing and rent prices and causes traffic snarls, cluttering views of the bay with construction cranes and workers in hard hats to more serious concerns such as red tide and the starvation of the manatees. Believed to be caused by climate change and some environmental spills, red tide, a harmful algal bloom known as *Karenia brevis*, has become an increasing hazard to the region's once pristine beaches and oceans. Along with killing fish and wildlife and generally being smelly, gross, and disgusting, in humans it also causes coughing; sneezing; shortness of breath; throat, eye, and skin irritation; and possibly asthma attacks. It comes and goes, and as of this writing, little effort has been made by the powers that be to find a solution.

The Florida Fish and Wildlife Conservation Commission, however, is working toward saving the beloved sea cow, providing them with life-sustaining lettuce and setting up manatee safety zones, among other steps. Decimated by pollution and loss of habitat, the sea grass essential to their survival is slowly being destroyed, resulting in nearly 2,000 deaths over the two-year period of 2021–2022. There is a bit of good news, however; the U.S. Fish and Wildlife Service estimates Florida's current population as 6,300, representing a significant increase over the past 25 years.

But with its gorgeous topography and (mostly) beautiful weather and beaches, Sarasota remains a welcoming, unpretentious jewel to artists and scholars, retirees and working people, tourists, snowbirds, transplants, and lifelong residents as it had with John and Charles Ringling when they purchased their first homes from Ralph Caples and John Thompson in 1911.

BIBLIOGRAPHY

Chapter 1

Barth, John, Jr. "The Origin of the Name, Sarasota." Sarasota
 History Alive! Accessed June 18, 2021. http://www.sarasota
 historyalive.com/index.php?src=directory&srctype=detail&
 refno=1589&category=Articles&view=history&back=history
 &submenu=home.

Barton, Jill. "Robotics Helps Revive Florida's Not-So-Ice
 Age." *LA Times*, February 16, 2003. https://www.latimes
 .com/archives/la-xpm-2003-feb-16-adna-icyfla16-story
 .html#:~:text=During%20the%20Ice%20Age%2C%20
 one,bigger%20perk%3A%20.virtually%20no%20humidity

Chapline, George F. "The Legend of Sara DeSoto." Sarasota
 History Alive! Accessed June 18, 2021. http://www.sarasota
 historyalive.com/index.php?src=directory&srctype=detail&
 refno=1337&category=Articles&view=history&back=history.

Exploring Florida. "The Calusa: 'The Shell Indians.'" Accessed
 June 18, 2021. https://fcit.usf.edu/florida/lessons/calusa/
 calusa1.htm#:~:text=The%20Calusa%20(kah%20LOOS%
 20ah,controlled%20most%20of%20south%20Florida.&text
 =The%20explorers%20soon%20became%20the,wrote%20
 home%20about%20in%201513.

Exploring Florida. "Tocobaga Indians of Tampa Bay." Accessed
 June 18, 2021. https://fcit.usf.edu/florida/lessons/tocobag/
 tocobag1.htm.

Grismer, Karl H. *The Story of Sarasota: The History of the City and
 County of Sarasota, Florida.* Sarasota, FL: M.E. Russell, 1946.

Hublin, Jean-Jacques, Nikolay Sirakov, Vera Aldeias, et al. "Initial Upper Palaeolithic *Homo sapiens* from Bacho Kiro Cave,

Bulgaria." *Nature* 581 (2020): 299–302. https://www.nature
.com/articles/s41586-020-2259-z.

LaHurd, Jeff. "Famed Sarasota Pageant Celebrated History, Real
and Imagined." *Sarasota Herald-Tribune*, April 28, 2013.
https://www.heraldtribune.com/story/news/2013/04/28/
famed-sarasota-pageant-celebrated-history-real-and-
imagined/29168979007/.

Milanich, Jerald. *Florida Indians and the Invasion from Europe.*
Gainesville, FL: University Press of Florida, 1998.

Swann, Brenda. "Florida's Native American Tribes, History and
Culture." Visit Florida. Accessed June 18, 2021. https://
www.visitflorida.com/travel-ideas/articles/arts-history
-native-american-culture-heritage-florida/.

Swanton, John. *Final Report of the United States: De Soto Expedition Commission.* Washington, DC: Smithsonian, 1985.

White, Susan Lynn. "The Florida Paleoindians." Sarasota
History Alive! Accessed June 18, 2021. http://www.sarasota
historyalive.com/index.php?src=directory&srctype=detail&
refno=1288&category=Articles&view=history&back=history
#:~:text=During%20the%20Paleoindian%20Period%20
(approximately,arid%20like%20an%20African%20savannah.

Chapter 2

Burger, Bill. "A Military Post on Sarasota Bay." Sarasota History
Alive! Accessed July 26, 2021. http://www.sarasotahistory
alive.com/index.php?back=history&src=directory&srctype
=detail&refno=1511&category=Articles&view=history.

Eger, Isaac. "A Newly Excavated Settlement Highlights Florida's
History as a Haven for Escaped Slaves." *Sarasota* magazine,
July 2018. https://www.sarasotamagazine.com/news-and
-profiles/2018/06/a-newly-excavated-settlement-highlights
-florida-s-history-as-a-haven-for-escaped-slaves.

Exploring Florida. "Transfer of Florida." Accessed July 26, 2021.
https://fcit.usf.edu/florida/lessons/trnsfer/trnsfer1.htm.

Favorite, Merab. "The First Settler." *Bradenton Times*, November 12, 2017. https://thebradentontimes.com/sunday-favorites -the-first-settler-p19239-133.htm.

Feldberg, Michael. "Judah Benjamin (1811-1884)." Jewish Virtual Library. Accessed July 26, 2021. https://www.jewish virtuallibrary.org/judah-benjamin.

Grismer, Karl H. *The Story of Sarasota: The History of the City and County of Sarasota, Florida.* Sarasota, FL: M.E. Russell, 1946.

Kipling, Kay. "Pioneer Mary Jane Wyatt Whitaker Braved the Wild and Helped Found a Dynasty." *Sarasota* magazine, July 27, 2020. https://www.sarasotamagazine.com/news-and -profiles/2020/07/mary-jane-wyatt-whitaker-braved-the -wilds-and-helped-to-found-a-dynasty.

Kleinberg, Eliot. "The Most Expensive War the White Man Ever Waged against Native Americans." *Sarasota Herald-Tribune*, February 27, 2019. https://www.heraldtribune.com/story/ lifestyle/things-to-do/destin/2019/02/28/florida-history -most-expensive-war-white-man-ever-waged-against-native -americans/5799219007/.

McDuffee, Lillie B. *The Lures of Manatee: A True Story of South Florida's Glamourous Past.* Sarasota, FL: Arcade Lithograph- ing, 1967.

Sarasota History Alive! "Frank and Matilda Binz House." Accessed July 26, 2021. http://www.sarasotahistoryalive.com/ index.php?src=directory&srctype=detail&refno=734& category=Buildings&view=history&back=history.

Smith, Mark D. "Creation of the Judah P. Benjamin Marker." Sarasota History Alive! Accessed July 26, 2021. http://www .sarasotahistoryalive.com/index.php?src=directory&srctype =detail&refno=1397&category=Articles&view=history& back=history.

Stinemetz, Morgan. "Legal Slavery Was Once a Part of County Life." *Sarasota Herald-Tribune*, March 1, 2004.

https://www.heraldtribune.com/story/news/2004/03/01/
legal-slavery-was-once-a-part-of-county-life/28790925007/.

Chapter 3

"An Assassination Society." *The New York Times*, February 1,
1885.

Bubil, Harold. "A Century Ago, Bertha Palmer Changed the
Region. *Sarasota Herald-Tribune*, January 17, 2010. https://
www.heraldtribune.com/story/news/2010/01/17/a-century
-ago-bertha-palmer-changed-the-region/28917822007/.

Cassell, Frank. *Suncoast Empire: Bertha Honore Palmer, Her
Family, and the Rise of Sarasota, 1910-1982*. Guilford, CT:
Pineapple, 2017.

Fanning, Timothy. "Assassins in Sarasota: How Secret Club
Killed City's First Postmaster." *TCPalm*, December 26, 2019.
https://www.tcpalm.com/story/news/newswire/2019/12/26/
assassins-secret-club-killed-florida-postmaster/2751961001/.

Favorite, Merab. "Newtown and Overtown." *Bradenton Times*,
February 12, 2017. https://thebradentontimes.com/sunday
-favorites-newtown-and-overtown-p18056-133.htm.

Favorite, Merab-Michal. "The Sarasota Assassination Society,
Part 2." *Bradenton Times*. Accessed April 20, 2023. https://
thebradentontimes.com/community-sunday-favorites-the
-sarasota-assassination-society-part-p11235-158.htm.

Florida Beef Council. "Cattle in Florida." Accessed September
10, 2021. https://www.floridabeef.org/raising-beef/cattle
-in-florida.

Florida State Parks. "Myakka River State Park." Accessed
September 10, 2021. https://www.floridastateparks.org/
parks-and-trails/myakka-river-state-park.

Grismer, Karl H. *The Story of Sarasota: The History of the City and
County of Sarasota, Florida*. Sarasota, FL: M.E. Russell, 1946.

Howard, Rosalyn, and Vickie Oldham. *Newtown Alive: Courage, Dignity, Determination*. Sarasota, FL: Newtown Conservation Historic District, 2017.

Kipling, Kay. "Emma E. Booker Taught Generations and Transformed Black Education in Sarasota." *Sarasota* magazine, June 22, 2020. https://www.sarasotamagazine.com/news -and-profiles/2020/06/to-mark-amendment-19-s-100th -anniversary-giving-women-the-right-to-vote-we-are-telling -stories-of-influential-women.

LaHurd, Jeff. "Legacy of Owen Burns." *Sarasota Herald-Tribune*, September 4, 2016. https://www.heraldtribune.com/news/ 20160904/legacy-of-owen-burns.

LaHurd, Jeff. *Sarasota: A History*. Charleston, SC: History Press, 2006.

LaHurd, Jeff. "Separate But Not Equal." Sarasota History Alive! Accessed September 10, 2021. http://www.sarasotahistory alive.com/index.php?src=directory&srctype=detail&refno =1352&category=Articles&view=history&back=history.

Lightfoot, Thomas Claude with Paula Benshoff. "Interview with Tom 'Cracker' Lightfoot." Manatee County Public Library historical collection, circa 1980.

Sarasota History Alive! "A. B. Edwards." Accessed September 10, 2021. http://www.sarasotahistoryalive.com/index.php?src =directory&srctype=detail&refno=1529&view=history&back =history.

Sarasota History Alive! "Crocker Memorial Church." Accessed September 10, 2021. http://www.sarasotahistoryalive.com/ index.php?src=directory&srctype=detail&refno=713& category=Buildings&view=history.

Sarasota History Alive! "Historic Spanish Point." Accessed September 10, 2021. http://www.sarasotahistoryalive.com/indcx .php?src=directory&srctype=detail&refno=844&category =markers&view=history&back=history&submenu=home.

Sarasota History Alive! "John Hamilton Gillespie." Accessed September 10, 2021. http://www.sarasotahistoryalive.com/ index.php?src=directory&srctype=detail&refno=846& category=Markers&view=history&back=history&submenu =home.

Sarasota History Alive! "Seaboard Railroad." Accessed September 10, 2021. http://www.sarasotahistoryalive.com/index .php?src=directory&srctype=detail&refno=875&category =Markers&view=history&back=history.

Shank, Ann. "Browning—An Early Sarasotan." Sarasota History Alive! Accessed September 10, 2021. http://www.sarasot ahistoryalive.com/index.php?src=directory&view=history& srctype=detail&refno=1361&category=Articles.

Smith, Jessi. "Bertha Palmer: The Woman Who Tamed Wild Sarasota." Visit Sarasota. December 31, 2020. Accessed September 10, 2021. https://www.visitsarasota.com/article/ bertha-palmer-woman-who-tamed-wild-sarasota.

Smith, Jessi. "Time-Traveler's Guide: A Brief History of Sarasota County." Visit Sarasota. Accessed September 10, 2021. https://www.visitsarasota.com/article/time-travelers-guide -brief-history-sarasota-county.

Weiser-Alexander, Kathy. "Cracker Cowmen." The Historical Society of Sarasota County. October 2018. https://hsosc .com/2021/02/10/cracker-cowmen.

Chapter 4

Ancestry.com. "Seventh Census of the United States," 1850. Census Place: Milwaukee Ward 1, Milwaukee, Wisconsin; Roll: M432_1003; Page: 181B; Image: 32.

Apps, Jerry. *Ringlingville USA: The Stupendous Story of Seven Siblings and Their Stunning Circus Success.* Wisconsin Historical Society Press, 2005.

Daubenberger, Gretchen. Untitled. *Palimpsest.* State Historical Society of Iowa, 1944, 184.

Plowden, Gene. *Those Amazing Ringlings and Their Circus.* New York, NY: Bonanza Books, 1967.

Ringling, Alfred. *Life Story of the Ringling Brothers: Illustrated; Humorous Incidents, Thrilling Trials, Many Hardships, and Ups and Downs, Telling How the Boys Built a Circus, and Showing the True Road to Success.* Chicago, IL: RR Donnelly & Sons, 1900.

Ringling Docents. "Points to Ponder, The Ringling Family." Accessed February 17, 2022. http://ringlingdocents.org/points-family.htm.

Ringling North, Henry, and Alden Hatch. *The Circus Kings: Our Ringling Family Story.* Garden City, NY: Doubleday & Company, 1960.

Weeks, David C. *Ringling: The Florida Years, 1911-1936.* University Press of Florida, 1993. Kindle.

Wisconsin Historical Society. "Alfred T. Ringling Was One of the Original Circusmen, Beginning His Career with the Famous Organization—Was Lover of Animals." Accessed April 20, 2023. https://www.wisconsinhistory.org/Records/Newspaper/BA2847.

Wisconsin Historical Society. "Bought First Circus Horse for Ringling." Accessed April 19, 2023. https://www.wisconsinhistory.org/Records/Newspaper/BA491.

Wisconsin Historical Society. "Old-Time Circus Boat Inspiration for Ringling Brothers 'Big Show.'" https://www.wisconsinhistory.org/Records/Newspaper/BA2849.

Wisconsin Historical Society. "Pa Ringling Made Buckets for State's First Fire Brigade." Accessed April 19, 2023. https://www.wisconsinhistory.org/Records/Newspaper/BA12110.

Wisconsin Historical Society. "Ringling [Rungeling], Albert 1852 1916." Accessed February 17, 2022. https://www.wisconsinhistory.org/Records/Article/CS12366.

Wisconsin Historical Society. "Ringling Show Had Start in Darlington." Accessed April 19, 2023. https://www.wisconsin history.org/Records/Newspaper/BA5816.

Wisconsin Historical Society. "Ringlings Once Lived in Rice Lake." Accessed April 19, 2023. https://www.wisconsin history.org/Records/Newspaper/BA2853.

Chapter 5

Ade, George. "The Big Top." *Builders*, July 20, 1957, 8.

Apps, Jerry. *Ringlingville USA: The Stupendous Story of Seven Siblings and Their Stunning Circus Success.* Wisconsin Historical Society Press, 2005.

Plowden, Gene. *Those Amazing Ringlings and Their Circus.* New York, NY: Bonanza Books, 1967.

Ringling North, Henry, and Alden Hatch. *The Circus Kings: Our Ringling Family Story.* Garden City, NY: Doubleday & Company, 1960.

Ritchie, Mark. "Do Hippopotamuses Actually Have Pink Sweat?" *Scientific American*, May 6, 2002. https://www .scientificamerican.com/article/do-hippopotamuses -actuall/#:~:text=HIPPOS%20spend%20most%20of%20 their,the%20fluid%20is%20not%20sweat.

Chapter 6

Apps, Jerry. *Ringlingville USA: The Stupendous Story of Seven Siblings and Their Stunning Circus Success.* Wisconsin Historical Society Press, 2005.

Bennett, James. "Sarasota Man Runs a Restaurant Out of an Old Ringling Train." *Sarasota Herald-Tribune*, August 8, 2019. https://www.heraldtribune.com/story/entertainment/dining/ 2019/08/08/sarasota man-runs-restaurant-out-of-old -ringling-train/4482691007/.

Buck, Pat Ringling. *The Ringling Legacy.* NP: PRB Enterprise, 1998.

Dreiblatt, Martha. *Brooklyn Daily Eagle*, July 14, 1929, 5.

Plowden, Gene. *Those Amazing Ringlings and Their Circus.* New York, NY: Bonanza Books, 1967.

Ringling North, Henry, and Alden Hatch. *The Circus Kings: Our Ringling Family Story.* Garden City, NY: Doubleday & Company, 1960.

Sauk County Historical Society. "Sauk County's National Historic Landmarks." Accessed May 8, 2022. https://saukcounty history.org/national-recognition.

Shank, Ann A. "Edith Ringling Was a Force behind the Circus." Sarasota History Alive! Accessed May 8, 2022. http://www .sarasotahistoryalive.com/index.php?src=directory&srctype =detail&refno=1153&category=Articles&view=history& back=history.

Shank, Ann A., and Mark D. Smith. "Caples Saw Potential in a Fishing Village." Sarasota History Alive! Accessed May 8, 2022. http://www.sarasotahistoryalive.com/index.php?src =directory&srctype=detail&refno=1305&category=Articles& view=history&back=history.

Weeks, David C. *Ringling: The Florida Years, 1911-1936.* University Press of Florida, 1993. Kindle.

Chapter 7

Florida Department of Transportation. "Development of Quality Assurance and Quality Control System for Post-Tensioned Segmental Bridges in Florida: Case of Ringling Bridge— Phase II, March 2019." Accessed July 17, 2022. https://fdot www.blob.core.windows.net/sitefinity/docs/default-source/ research/reports/fdot-bdv29-977-34-sum.pdf.

LaHurd, Jeff. "Beloved by Many, Charles Ringling Left Big Mark on Sarasota." *Sarasota Herald Tribune*, June 13, 2022. https://www.heraldtribune.com/story/news/history/ 2022/06/13/jeff-lahurd-legacy-beloved-mr-charlie-ringling -endures/9999962002/.

LaHurd, Jeff. "Breakfast and a Winter White House." Sarasota History Alive! Accessed July 17, 2022. http://www.sarasota historyalive.com/index.php?src=directory&srctype=detail& refno=1414&view=history&back=history.

LaHurd, Jeff. "Controversy, Thy Name Is Ringling Causeway Bridge." *Sarasota Herald-Tribune*, July 31, 2008. https://www .heraldtribune.com/story/news/2008/07/31/controversy-thy name-is-ringling-causeway-bridge/28651585007/.

LaHurd, Jeff. "Sarasota's First (Almost) Ritz-Carlton." *Sarasota Herald-Tribune*, December 5, 2021. https://www.herald tribune.com/story/news/history/2021/12/05/jeff-lahurd -sarasotas-failed-first-try-ritz-carlton-long-saga/882624500 2/.

LaHurd, Jeff. "Sarasota's Ringling Bridge Was Always a Symbol of City Progress." *Sarasota Herald-Tribune*, August 17, 2014. https://www.heraldtribune.com/story/news/2014/08/17/ sarasotas-ringling-bridge-was-always-a-symbol-of-city -progress/29265048007/.

McCarty, Ron. "Mable Burton Ringling." Sarasota History Alive! Accessed July 17, 2022. http://www.sarasotahistoryalive.com/ index.php?src=directory&srctype=detail&refno=1439&view =history&back=history.

Plowden, Gene. *Those Amazing Ringlings and Their Circus*. New York, NY: Bonanza Books, 1967.

"Ringling Can't Send Elephant for Republican Jubilee." *The New York Times*, April 28, 1929, 31.

"Ringling Causeway Plans Announced." *Sarasota Times*, January 3, 1924, 1.

Ringling North, Henry, and Alden Hatch. *The Circus Kings: Our Ringling Family Story*. Garden City, NY: Doubleday & Company, 1960.

Ritz-Carlton Sarasota. Accessed July 17, 2022. https://www .ritzcarlton.com/en/hotels/florida/sarasota.

"Sarasotans Aboard Yacht Here." *Sarasota Herald*, March 9, 1927, 1.

"Skeleton at the Ritz Carlton." Ringling Archives. *Key Notes*, 1953.

St. Armands Circle History. Accessed July 17, 2022. [website defunct] https://starmandscircleassoc.com/st-armands-circle-history/.

Weeks, David C. *Ringling: The Florida Years, 1911-1936.* University Press of Florida, 1993. Kindle.

Chapter 8

Binney, Marcus. "Ca' d'Zan, Sarasota, Florida." *Country Life* 160 (1976): 1202–05.

Bohler, Julius W. *John Ringling: Builder and Collector.* Sarasota, FL: The John and Mable Ringling Museum of Art, 1949.

Chachere, Vickie. "Circus Magnate's Home Refurbished to Its Former Glory." *South Florida Sun-Sentinel*, May 13, 2002. https://www.sun-sentinel.com/travel/sfl-512ringling museum-story.html.

Clarke, Gerald. "Florida's Ca d'Zan." *Architectural Digest* 59, no. 10 (2002): 206–15.

De Groft, Aaron H. "John Ringling in *Perpetua Memoria*: The Legacy and Prestige of Art and Collecting." PhD diss. Florida State University, 2000.

De Groft, Aaron H., and David C. Weeks. *Ca' d'Zan: Inside the Ringling Mansion.* Sarasota, FL: John and Mable Ringling Museum of Art, 2004.

Grismer, Karl H. *The Story of Sarasota: The History of the City and County of Sarasota, Florida.* Sarasota, FL: M.E. Russell, 1946.

Kruse, Michael. "John Ringling Set the Tone for the Sarasota of Today." *Sarasota* magazine, March 2, 2015. https://www.sarasotamagazine.com/arts-and-entertainment/2015/03/john-ringling-sarasota.

Martha G. "History of Madison Square Garden." *ExperienceFirst* (blog). Accessed September 11, 2022. https://www.exp1 .com/blog/untold-nyc-history-madison-square-garden/.

Meter, Amanda Ellen. "John Ringling: Story of a Capitalist." Master's thesis. Florida State University, 2009.

Murray, Marian. *Cà d'Zan: The House That John and Mable Ringling Built, A Short Guide to the Ringling Residence.* Sarasota, FL: Ringling Museum, 1952.

Ormond, Mark, ed. *John Ringling: Dreamer, Builder, Collector.* Sarasota, FL: John and Mable Ringling Museum, 1996.

Pecky Cypress and More. "What Is Pecky Cypress?" Accessed September 11, 2022. https://www.peckycypressandmore .com/what-is-pecky-cypress.html.

The Ringling. "Bayfront Gardens." Accessed September 11, 2022. https://www.ringling.org/events/venue/bayfront-gardens.

The Ringling. "Ca' d'Zan." Accessed September 11, 2022. https:// www.ringling.org/ca-dzan.

The Ringling. "Ca' d'Zan First Floor Audio Tour." Accessed September 11, 2022. https://www.ringling.org/sites/default/files/ Ca-Audio-Tour-Transcript.pdf.

The Ringling. "History of the Ringling." Accessed September 11, 2022. https://www.ringling.org/history-ringling.

The Ringling. "The Ringling Receives $1.5 Million Grant to Restore the Ca'd'Zan's Organ." Accessed September 11, 2022. https://www.ringling.org/ringling-receives-15-million -grant-restore-ca%E2%80%99d%E2%80%99zan%E2%80% 99s-organ.

Ringling: Collector and Builder in the Ringling Museums: A Magnificent Gift to the State of Florida. Sarasota, FL: The John and Mable Ringling Museum of Art, 1952.

Ringling North, Henry, and Alden Hatch. *The Circus Kings: Our Ringling Family Story.* Garden City, NY: Doubleday & Company, 1960.

Scalera, Michelle A. *Cà d'Zan: The Restoration of the Ringling Mansion*. Edited by Deborah W. Walk. Sarasota, FL: John and Mable Ringling Museum of Art, 2006.

Sightseeing Tours Italy. "What Are Different Styles of Architecture in Venice? Accessed September 11, 2022. https://www.venicetoursitaly.it/blog/what-are-different-styles-of-architecture-in-venice/.

Weeks, David C. *Ringling: The Florida Years, 1911-1936*. University Press of Florida, 1993. Kindle.

Wernick, Robert. "The Greatest Show on Earth Didn't Compare to Home." *Smithsonian* (1981, September 23): 62–71.

Chapter 9

Conforti, Michael. "The Astor Rooms." In *John Ringling: Dreamer, Builder, Collector*, edited by Mark Ormond, 127–38. Sarasota FL: John and Mable Ringling Museum, 1996.

De Groft, Aaron H. "John Ringling in *Perpetua Memoria*: The Legacy and Prestige of Art and Collecting." PhD diss. Florida State University, 2000.

Ewing, Heather. "Early Perceptions of the Museum." In *John Ringling: Dreamer, Builder, Collector*, edited by Mark Ormond, 26–42. Sarasota, FL: John and Mable Ringling Museum, 1996.

Florida State University Libraries. "John Ringling: Art Collector." October 21, 2022. https://guides.lib.fsu.edu/john-ringling-art-collector.

Meter, Amanda Ellen. "John Ringling: Story of a Capitalist." Master's thesis. Florida State University, 2009.

The Ringling. "Collections." Accessed October 21, 2022. https://ringling.org/collections#:~:text=The%20Museum's%20collection%20includes%20more,twentieth%20and%20twenty-first%20centuries.

The Ringling. "The Gathering of the Manna." Accessed October 21, 2022. https://emuseum.ringling.org/objects/22512/the-gathering-of-the-manna.

The Ringling. "Museum of Art." Accessed October 21, 2022. https://www.ringling.org/museum-art.

Weeks, David C. *Ringling: The Florida Years, 1911–1936*. University Press of Florida, 1993. Kindle.

Wetenhall, John. *A Museum Once Forgotten: Rebirth of the John and Mable Ringling Museum of Art*. Sarasota, FL: John and Mable Ringling Museum of Art, 2007.

Zafran, Eric. "John and Lulu." In *John Ringling: Dreamer, Builder, Collector*, edited by Mark Ormond, 43–55. Sarasota, FL: John and Mable Ringling Museum, 1996.

Chapter 10

Airbnb. "Historic Cottage in Downtown Sarasota." Accessed December 19, 2022. https://www.airbnb.com/rooms/602154857519991855?source_impression_id=p3_1678033682_gS9ZdR8xxNc3sK4x.

DiCesare, Frank. "Sarasota County and the American Clown: A 100-Year Relationship." Visit Sarasota. Accessed December 19, 2022. https://www.visitsarasota.com/article/sarasota-county-and-american-clown-100-year-relationship.

Favorite, Merab-Michal, and Drew Winchester. "Sunday Favorites: Welcome to 'Midget City.'" *Bradenton Times*, nd. https://thebradentontimes.com/sunday-favorites-welcome-to-midget-city-p2045-158.htm.

Fottler, Marsha. "Sarasota 'Midget's House' Has Quite a Story." *Sarasota Herald-Tribune*, May 25, 2012. https://www.heraldtribune.com/story/business/real-estate/2012/05/25/sarasota-midgets-house-has-quite-a-story/29100416007/.

Gordon, Emmanuel Taylor. *Born to Be*. Lincoln, NE: University of Nebraska Press, 1995.

History Channel. "Fire Engulfs Circus Big Top in Hartford, Killing 167." Accessed December 19, 2022. https://www.history.com/this-day-in-history/hartford-circus-fire.

LaHurd, Jeff. "Wealth on the Line, Ringling Made Sarasota the Circus City." *Sarasota Herald-Tribune*, March 7, 2022. https://www.heraldtribune.com/story/business/real-estate/2022/03/07/jeff-lahurd-how-and-why-sarasota-became-circus-city/9333161002/.

Leffel, Tim. "Freak Shows and Farces at the Ringling Circus Museum in Sarasota." *Perceptive Travel* (blog), n.d. https://www.perceptivetravel.com/issues/0922/sarasota.html.

Newspapers.com. "Swiss Giantess, Exhibited to the King with Caroline Crachami in 1824." Accessed April 19, 2023. https://www.newspapers.com/clip/28801979/swiss-giantess-exhibited-to-the-king/.

Perkins, Robert E. *The First Fifty Years: Ringling School of Art and Design, Sarasota, Florida, 1931-1981*. Sarasota, FL: Ringling School of Art Library Association, 1982.

Phone Interview by author with Murray Horwitz, December 16, 2022.

Phone Interview by author with Peggy Williams, November 21, 2022.

Plowden, Gene. *Those Amazing Ringlings and Their Circus*. New York, NY: Bonanza Books, 1967.

The Ringling. "Art Library." Accessed December 19, 2022. https://www.ringling.org/art-library-0.

The Ringling. "Historic Asolo Theater." Accessed December 19, 2022. https://www.ringling.org/historic-asolo-theater.

The Ringling. "History of the Circus Museum." Accessed December 19, 2022. https://www.ringling.org/history-circus museum.

The Ringling. "The Ringling's First Director Part One: Chick Austin Arrives at the Ringling." Accessed December 19,

2022. https://www.ringling.org/ringlings-first-director-part
-one-chick-austin-arrives-ringling.

The Ringling. "The Ringling's First Director Part Three: Chick
Austin's Ringling Legacy." Accessed December 19, 2022.
https://www.ringling.org/ringlings-first-director-part-three
-chick-austins-ringling-legacy.

Ringling College of Art and Design. "About Us." Accessed
December 19, 2022. https://www.ringling.edu/
about/#:~:text=The%20art%20school%20separated%20
from,)%20on%20December%2011%2C%201979.

Ringling North, Henry, and Alden Hatch. *The Circus Kings: Our
Ringling Family Story*. Garden City, NY: Doubleday & Company, 1960.

Sarasota History Alive! "Circus in Venice." Accessed December
19, 2022. http://www.sarasotahistoryalive.com/index.php?src
=directory&srctype=detail&refno=830&category=Markers&
view=history&back=history.

Shepley Bulfinch. "This Library's an Open Book." Accessed
December 19, 2022. https://shepleybulfinch.com/projects/
ringling-college-of-art-and-design-alfred-r-goldstein-
library/.

Wallenfeldt, Jeff. "Ringling Bros. and Barnum & Bailey Circus."
Brittanica.com. Accessed December 19, 2022. https://www
.britannica.com/topic/Ringling-Bros-and-Barnum-and
-Bailey-Combined-Shows.

Weeklies, Kent. "Kaleidoscope: End of an Era, Many Will Miss
Ringling Circus." *Akron Beacon Journal*, February 4, 2017.
https://www.beaconjournal.com/story/news/local/hudson
-hubtimes/2017/02/05/kaleidoscope-end-era-many-will/
19977921007/.

Weeks, David C. *Ringling: The Florida Years, 1911-1936*. University Press of Florida, 1993. Kindle.

Chapter 11

De Groft, Aaron H., and David C. Weeks. *Ca' d'Zan: Inside the Ringling Mansion*. Sarasota, FL: John and Mable Ringling Museum of Art, 2004.

Johnston, Alva. "Boss of the Circus." *Reader's Digest*, July 1933, 49.

LaHurd, Jeff. "He Made So Many Smiles But Had So Few of His Own." *Sarasota Herald-Tribune*, July 29, 2013. https://www.heraldtribune.com/story/news/2013/07/29/he-made-so-many-smiles-but-had-so-few-of-his-own/29189929007/.

Plowden, Gene. *Those Amazing Ringlings and Their Circus*. New York, NY: Bonanza Books, 1967.

Plunket, Robert. "The Lavish Life and Forgotten Legacy of John Ringling North." *Sarasota* magazine, July 26, 2018. https://www.sarasotamagazine.com/news-and-profiles/2018/07/john-ringling-north.

Ringling Docents. "Ringling's Second Marriage a 'Three Ring Circus.'" Accessed April 19, 2023. http://ringlingdocents.org/emily.htm.

Ringling North, Henry, and Alden Hatch. *The Circus Kings: Our Ringling Family Story*. Garden City, NY: Doubleday & Company, 1960.

Sarasota History Alive! "Samuel Gumpertz House." Accessed January 19, 2023. http://www.sarasotahistoryalive.com/index.php?src=directory&srctype=detail&refno=1082&view=history&back=history.

Weeks, David C. *Ringling: The Florida Years, 1911-1936*. University Press of Florida, 1993. Kindle.

Chapter 12

Britannica.com. "Circus: Theatrical Entertainment." Accessed March 4, 2023. https://www.britannica.com/art/circus-theatrical-entertainment.

Cappiello, Julie. "9 Facts about Animal Circuses You Should Know." *Animals in the Wild* (blog), June 22, 2020. https://www.worldanimalprotection.us/blogs/9-facts-about-animal-circuses-you-should-know.

The Circus Arts Conservatory. "More Than a Circus for 25 Years!" Accessed March 4, 2023. https://circusarts.org.

Cirque Italia. "Dive into the Magical World of Cirque!" Accessed March 4, 2023. https://cirqueitalia.com/.

Davis, Janet M. "America's Big Circus Spectacular Has a Long and Cherished History." *Smithsonian Magazine*, March 22, 2017. https://www.smithsonianmag.com/history/americas-big-circus-spectacular-has-long-and-cherished-history-180962621/.

Feld Entertainment. "Uplifting. Unifying. Unforgettable. Nothing Lives Up to Seeing It Live." Accessed March 4, 2023. https://www.feldentertainment.com/productions/.

Florida Fish and Wildlife Conservation Commission. "How Can I Help?" Accessed March 4, 2023. https://myfwc.com/wildlifehabitats/wildlife/manatee/myfwccomhow-to-help/#:~:text=You%20can%20help%20protect%20manatees%20in%20many%20ways.&text=Report%20injured%2C%20orphaned%2C%20entangled%2C,(s)%20can%20be%20saved.

Gibson, Kate. "Ringling Brothers Circus to Relaunch—Without Animal Acts." CBS News, May 18, 2022. https://www.cbsnews.com/news/ringling-brothers-greatest-show-on-earth-animal-acts-elephants-disney-on-ice/.

Gibtown Showmans Club. "Trade Show and Extravaganza." Accessed March 4, 2023. https://gibtownshowmensclub.com/.

"John Ringling Dies of Pneumonia." *The New York Times*, December 2, 1936, 27.

LaHurd, Jeff. "Who Is Buried in John Ringling's Tomb?" *Sarasota Herald-Tribune*, May 28, 2017. https://www

.heraldtribune.com/story/news/local/sarasota/2017/05/28/
who-is-buried-in-john-ringlings-tomb/20773707007/.

Marie Selby Botanical Gardens. "A History of Marie Selby
Botanical Gardens." Accessed March 4, 2023. https://selby
.org/about/history/#:~:text=Shortly%20after%20completing
%20her%20musical,First%20Presbyterian%20Church%20
of%20Marietta.

Marie Selby Botanical Gardens. "Marie Selby Botanical Gardens." Accessed March 4, 2023. https://selby.org/.

Meter, Amanda Ellen. "John Ringling: Story of a Capitalist."
Master's thesis. Florida State University, 2009.

Norton Center. "About the Van Wezel." Accessed March 4, 2023.
https://nortoncenter.com/wpcontent/uploads/2019/09/
PETERS-the-Van-Wezel.pdf.

Official Marietta Museum of Art and Whimsy. "The Whimsy
Museum and Lee Family Gardens Are Open." Accessed
March 4, 2023. http://www.whimsymuseum.org/.

"Ringling Feud Delays Burial for 55 Years." *Tampa Bay Times*.
Published June 6, 1991. Updated October 13, 2005. https://
www.tampabay.com/archive/1991/06/06/ringling-feud
-delays-burial-for-55-years/.

Royal Hanneford Circus. "Be a Part of Our History." Accessed
March 4, 2023. https://royalhannefordcircus.com/.

"Sarasota Mourns Him." *The New York Times*, December 3, 1936,
25.

U.S. Fish and Wildlife Service. "Manatee." Accessed March 4,
2023. https://www.fws.gov/species/manatee-trichechus
-manatus.

Variety Attractions. "Zerbini Circus." Accessed March 4, 2023.
https://zerbinifamilycircus.com/.

Weeks, David C. *Ringling: The Florida Years, 1911–1936.* Univer
sity Press of Florida, 1993. Kindle.

INDEX

Page references for images and textboxes are italicized.

ABOUT THE AUTHOR

Sandra Gurvis (www.sandragurvis.com) is the author of eigh-
teen commercially published books and hundreds of magazine
articles. Her titles include *Myths and Mysteries of Ohio*, *Day Trips
from Columbus* (third edition), *Ohio Curiosities* (second edition),
Careers for Nonconformists (a selection of the Quality Paperback
Book Club), and more. Along with having her books featured on
radio and television and in print and online, her biography, *Paris
Hilton*, has been translated into Chinese. Her newest nonfiction
title is *111 Places in Columbus That You Must Not Miss*.

Sandra is the author of two novels. *The Pipe Dreamers* (reissued
in 2020) is about the Vietnam protests of the late 1960s and early
1970s, mostly set in a small Ohio college town, and *Country Club
Wives*, a satire on women, money, and homeless animals in "New
Albany, oops, New Wellington, Ohio," which was optioned as a
television series by Insight Productions out of Toronto, Canada.

A freelance writer for over 40 years, Sandra has written cor-
porate profiles and technical articles and created web content for
clients such as Ohio State University Wexner Medical Center,
Merrill Lynch, Council for Advancement and Support of Education (CASE), and Association of American Medical Colleges
(AAMC). In addition to rewriting and editing books on medical
and business topics, she prepares newsletters and assists in the creation of printed and web content on a variety of health care and
business issues.

Along with being selected for residencies and fellowships at
the Mary Anderson Center in Mt. St. Francis, Indiana, and the
Vermont Writers Studio in Johnston and receiving grants from
the National Institute for Health Care Management (NIHCM)
and the LBJ Library in Austin, Texas, as well as certification from
the American Medical Writers Association (AMWA), Sandra is

a longtime member of the American Society of Journalists and Authors (ASJA). She lives in Bradenton, Florida, and is currently working on *Doing Hard Time in Geezerville*, the first of a trio of satires/mysteries set in the Villages in Florida.